EUROPEAN MONOGRAPHS IN SOCIAL PSYCHOLOGY 31
Series Editor: HENRI TAJFEL

The Power of Minorities

GABRIEL MUGNY

*Faculté de Psychologie et des Sciences
de l'Education
Université de Genève*

In collaboration with Stamos Papastamou
Translated from the French by Carol Sherrard

1982

Published in cooperation with
EUROPEAN ASSOCIATION OF EXPERIMENTAL
SOCIAL PSYCHOLOGY
by
ACADEMIC PRESS
A Subsidiary of Harcourt Brace Jovanovich, Publishers
London   New York
Paris   San Diego   San Francisco   São Paulo
Sydney   Tokyo   Toronto

ACADEMIC PRESS INC. (LONDON) LTD.
24/28 Oval Road
London NW1

United States Edition published by
ACADEMIC PRESS INC.
111 Fifth Avenue
New York, New York 10003

British Library Cataloguing in Publication Data

Mugny, Gabriel
   The power of minorities.—(European
   monographs in social psychology; 31)
   1. Minorities—Europe
   I. Title   II. Papastamou, Stamos
   III. Series
   305'.094 (expanded)   HN380.Z9M/

   ISBN 0–12–509720–4

   LCCCN 82–71017

Photoset by
Paston Press, Norwich
Printed in Great Britain by
St Edmundsbury Press,
Bury St Edmunds,
Suffolk

The Power of Minorities

This is a volume in
EUROPEAN MONOGRAPHS IN SOCIAL PSYCHOLOGY

Series Editor: Henri Tajfel

European Monographs in Social Psychology

Series Editor: HENRI TAJFEL

E. A. CARSWELL and R. ROMMETVEIT (*eds*)
Social Contexts of Messages, 1971

J. ISRAEL and H. TAJFEL (*eds*)
The Context of Social Psychology: A Critical Assessment, 1972

J. R. EISER and W. STROEBE
Categorization and Social Judgement, 1972

M. VON CRANACH and I. VINE (*eds*)
Social Communication and Movement: Studies of Interaction and Expression in Man
   and Chimpanzee, 1973

C. HERZLICH
Health and Illness: A Social Psychological Analysis, 1973

J. M. NUTTIN, JR
The Illusion of Attitude Change: Towards a Response Contagion Theory of Persuasion,
   1975

H. GILES and P. F. POWESLAND
Speech Style and Social Evaluation, 1975

J. K. CHADWICK-JONES
Social Exchange Theory: Its Structure and Influence in Social Psychology, 1976

M. BILLIG
Social Psychology and Intergroup Relations, 1976

S. MOSCOVICI
Social Influence and Social Change, 1976

R. SANDELL
Linguistic Style and Persuasion, 1977

A. HEENWOLD
Decoding Oral Language, 1978

H. GILES (*ed*)
Language, Ethnicity and Intergroup Relations, 1977

H. TAJFEL (*ed*)
Differentiation between Social Groups: Studies in the Social Psychology of Intergroup
   Relations, 1978

M. BILLIG
Fascists: A Social Psychological View of the National Front, 1978

C. P. WILSON
Jokes, Form, Content, Use and Function, 1979

J. P. FORGAS
Social Episodes: The Study of Interaction Routines, 1979

R. A. HINDE
Towards Understanding Relationships, 1979

A-N. PERRET-CLERMONT
Social Interaction and Cognitive Development in Children, 1980

B. A. GEBER and S. P. NEWMAN
Soweto's Children: The Development of Attitudes, 1980

S. H. NG
The Social Psychology of Power, 1980

P. SCHÖNBACH, P. GOLLWITZER, G. STIEPEL and U. WAGNER
Education and Intergroup Attitudes, 1981

C. ANTAKI (*ed*)
The Psychology of Ordinary Explanations of Social Behaviour, 1981

W. P. ROBINSON (*ed*)
Communication in Development, 1981

H. BRANDSTÄTTER, J. H. DAVIS and G. STOCK-KREICHGAUER (*eds*)
Group Decision Making

J. P. FORGAS (*ed*)
Social Cognition: Perspectives in Everyday Understanding

H. T. HIMMELWEIT, P. HUMPHREYS, M. JAEGER and M. KATZ
How Voters Decide: A Longitudinal Study of Political Attitudes extending over Fifteen
 Years

P. STRINGER (*ed*)
Confronting Social Issues: Applications of Social Psychology, Vol. 1

In preparation
P. STRINGER (*ed*)
Confronting Social Issues: Applications of Social Psychology, Vol. 2

M. VON CRANACH
Goal-Directed Action

J. JASPERS, F. FINCHAM and M. HEWSTONE
Attribution Theory and Research: Conceptual, Developmental and Social Dimensions

Foreword

Slowly but surely, the psychology of active minorities is beginning to be better known. This original book is the proof of it. When we ourselves began this type of work, many social psychologists saw it as the desire to be original at all costs or as the adoption of a subject merely because it had been overlooked by everyone else. Although the desire to be original is not a reprehensible motive in research, those who imputed it to us took it upon themselves to transform the objective and theoretical reasons motivating this interest in minorities in society into the subjective reasons of particular individuals. After all, there are still plenty of other uncharted areas on the map of social psychology! If the question relating to this form of influence is somewhat sharply put, it is, firstly, because the dominant theory has shown itself to be incapable of explaining social change and innovation and, secondly, because it is has ended up in a cul-de-sac. How has this come about?

As is well known, the dominant theory is based on the notion that individuals and groups *adapt* themselves to reality. In their efforts to adapt, each person tries to exercise correct judgement and to acquire certainties about the properties of objects, the behaviour of people, and so on. The individual who is not able to do this alone will look to others, seeking their help in order to know what to see and what to think. Because several heads are better than one, the individual is open to influence; to adopt the viewpoint of the majority becomes the equivalent of exercising correct judgement.

There is another version of the same idea: deviants are an obstacle to the group's efforts to adapt to reality and carry out its aims. By exerting pressure on deviants and changing their judgements or opinions, the group removes this obstacle and attains its own ends, once unanimity has been restored. In sum, conformity is indispensable to the internal dynamics of all social structures. This is certainly true, but ceases to be so as soon as it is maintained that conformity alone is necessary. This

ix

was realized quite early, because among the thousands of experiments done to verify the various aspects of the theory based on this postulate, a certain number produced worrying results. For instance, when people in groups were asked to find the best solution to a problem and were told that they would be rewarded in proportion to the quality of the solution, it was found that most individuals still chose majority solutions. Furthermore, they continued to conform to the majority even when it was clear that by doing so the group would lose. It was also noticed that even if an individual is strongly induced to give the correct solution or is altered to the incorrectness of a particular judgement, that individual will, as soon as other persons are present, nevertheless choose to respond in the same way as these others. This, then, is how the cul-de-sac is reached: conformity does not always play a positive role, since the group may suffer because of it. In the social adaptation to reality, other people not only have a positive influence; they may also have a negative influence. Milgram's dramatic experiments on obedience to authority demonstrated just this point in a kind of experimental firework display.

Once this impasse was reached, research on social influence declined steeply, and analysis of the phenomenon has now been abandoned. This is entirely understandable; for a proper analysis it would have been necessary to explain how it is that the deviant resists, and tries to change the group, only in order to attain goals from which the majority recoil. The existing theory did not allow such questions to be raised; in fact they were explicitly excluded. It so happens, as we have already indicated, that all of these questions are to do with innovation, the action of a minority (which may sometimes be reduced to an individual). This was the starting-point of our own research in this area, in the hope of finding a way out of the impasse and engaging with a new set of phenomena. We believe we have fulfilled this hope.

Nevertheless, we have not managed to convince others, despite the time we have spent on it, that the study of social change and resistance to conformity pressure is necessarily the study of the psychology of active minorities. Instead, it is imagined that a collectivity is able to change by itself through a non-conflictual consultation of conscience, or by virtue of a general law, with no occurrence of conflict or deviance. This is a fundamental error, and reality has always shown it to be so. More than that, it is an impossibility, because of a kind of social Gödel's theorem. It is held that a social system changes according to the laws of its own internal development; it is supposed that all the people included within it belong to it, and that the system is able to encompass and define everyone included within it. According to Gödel's theorem, a system includes propositions for which it cannot, itself, provide the proof. These propositions can only be proved if another system is created. If the system changes, it is because the non-demonstrable propositions are in search of an alternative system, and it is these which initiate the change. It follows that there cannot be any social system without deviance or without active minorities, any more than there could be a system which could provide proofs of all the propositions to which it gives rise, unles it contains some hidden paradox. It also follows that even if change in a social system conforms to general laws, its immediate and obvious cause is the existence and action of minorities. Without these general laws there will be no system; without these minorities there will be no social change.

Gabriel Mugny has been among the first to have understood this viewpoint, and this must be greatly to his credit because there are obvious risks for a young academic in pursuing genuinely original research. However, the idea which has captivated him is still more important. What he has brought to our attention is that if we want to understand the strategies of minorities (which are consistent by definition—otherwise they would not be minorities), we must distinguish between two modes of action. One is a strategy of negotiation, and the other is a strategy of rigidity or inflexibility in the choice of options. To simplify this and make it more concrete, we can say that the first is a "reformist" socialist strategy while the second is "leftist". There is also a third strategy, which consists in keeping both irons in the fire and using sometimes one, sometimes the other.

This example will give us a backcloth against which we can appreciate the real significance of the behavioural styles defined by Mugny. These styles will interest all those who are concerned with politics, collective decision-making, and mass communications. Most of the ingenious and persuasive experiments in this book show directly how these styles operate and have their effects. Here we have a solid body of results which social psychology must reckon with. There has been real progression from the first experiment with Blaise Pierrehumbert and Rosita Zubel, following in the path laid out by Ricateau, whose research talents we sorely miss. But it has needed tenacity, enthusiasm, and imagination to follow this path—all qualities possessed by Gabriel Mugny.

This research has built for us a picture of a new phenomenon: influence is exerted by minorities, and the attitude changes it brings about are indirect. More specifically, people are not convinced by the immediate content of the minority "message"; they resist it because they fear that they would themselves be seen as deviants if they were to adopt the minority position. This resistance has the effect of displacing the effect of the "message" on to related, contiguous attitudes and opinions. For instance, one would not accept that there is real danger from nuclear power, but one would accept that there should be democratic control of nuclear installations, or vice versa. In effect, when confronted with an opposed majority one complies without being convinced; when confronted with an opposed minority one is convinced without complying. This phenomenon has been explored and confirmed beyond question by Mugny together with Papastamou, who has now joined the team of social psychologists set up in Geneva by Willem Doise. From now on anyone interested in attitude and opinion change or in the effects of mass communications will have to use two measures in assessing the effects of an influence agent: one of direct change and one of indirect change. Separately, these measures have no interest: it is only the difference or "tension" between them which has psychological significance.

Of all the research reported in this book there is one study in particular which I recommend to the reader's attention, with the same discreet pleasure that one connoisseur of wine has in recommending a fine but little-known local wine to another connoisseur: this is the study of personalization. Although it does not have as much body as I would like or the sobriety of explication ideally desired, it does open up possibilities that leave one anxious and perplexed about the psychological means we appear to have available for devaluing and weakening the impact of minorities. It is a common experience to see an issue of principle and objective content transformed into one which is instead focused on persons and thus rendered arbitrary and subjective. Once this has happened, the issue is no longer seen as a matter of truth but one of power. It is a somewhat less common experience, though none the less significant for that, to see the victims transformed, by virtue of their very weakness, into the cause of the injustices they suffer and the oppressions that are forced upon them. Some people believed, for instance, that the victims of concentration camps were responsible for their own numberless sufferings, through inadvertence or disrespect of the law. But this happens everywhere—in families, among respectable academics, as I have recently had occasion to observe, and among politicians. All of this is to be understood in relation to this process of psychologization. It consists in nullifying an argument, ignoring a true proposition, weakening a group, and deflecting interest from the object onto the subject; to achieve all this, it is sufficient to present as having a psychological or personal origin something which does not in truth have this origin. The criminalization and psychiatrization of dissidents have their place in this strategy: not as a means of silencing individuals so much as of silencing and discrediting ideas.

All of this, you may say, is as old as Methuselah. Yet there are plenty of things even older than Methuselah which we have not yet understood. As soon as we make the effort to understand them, they are no longer the same, and, what is more, they are suddenly rejuvenated. Read this book, however, and you will see for yourself. I hope that if you are intrigued by this research, you will not hesitate to continue it yourself; the discovery of Mugny and Papastamou is a gold mine awaiting exploration.

These, then, are the three great insights of this research: styles of behaviour, negotiating or rigid; the nature of influence effects, direct or indirect; and psychologization. This work contains plenty of other discoveries and presents them clearly. Reading it, one can sense hard work and a great deal of enthusiasm. I hope that it will attract the readers it deserves, and I am sure that they will be enriched by it, both in their ideas and, eventually, in their practice.

Serge Moscovici

Acknowledgement

Stamos Papastamou has contributed widely to the experimental illustration of the theory proposed in this book. He is presently *maître-assistant* (research associate) at the Faculty of Psychology and Educational Psychology of the University of Geneva.

Contents

Part Two
EXPERIMENTAL ILLUSTRATION

Part One

The Social Psychology of
Minority Influence

Introduction

1. Which social psychology?

A scientific discipline does not see itself as being defined by its methods, any more than it sees itself as limited by the phenomena it studies. Its methods do no more than specify lines of approach, and the phenomena it chooses to study only indicate which matters are of interest at a given, and sometimes short-lived, moment in its history.

We, then, shall not seek to define social psychology by its methods (even though we favour one of them, experimentation) or by its objects of study (of which social influence is one). We shall define it rather by its theoretical approach to the phenomena it studies, that is to say by the nature of the explanations which it offers, or more exactly should offer.

Social psychology, like the other social sciences, is currently in a state of crisis. Specifically, it has to meet two major criticisms (Doise *et al.*, 1978). One accuses it of artificiality in the experimental situations dreamed up by its practitioners. The other, perhaps more serious, accuses it of furnishing scientific support to the dominant ideology. We should like to offer here a definition of social psychology which will not only be more satisfying but also allow it to escape these criticisms. We shall give a detailed description of what such a definition can bring to the conceptualization of a particular phenomenon: the influence of minorities. If this attempt succeeds, it will be the best argument in favour of social psychology.

The crisis in social psychology (as in other disciplines) has come about because the nature of the explanations offered differs according to the school of social psychologists. These fail to make contact on even a single principle of explanation; some dominate, while others (active minorities?) are seen as "deviants" in their efforts to impose their own explanatory principles. Naturally some of them will abandon the field of battle for different territories, open to new ideas. Our choice has been to join battle instead, over the issue of social influence processes. Let us begin by defining them.

2. Social influence in the "strict" sense

In the most specific accepted meaning, social influence processes can be defined as modifications (or restructurings) of perceptions, judgements, opinions, behaviours, etc., which are observable (and measurable according to specific techniques) at the level of individuals. These transformations result from the knowledge which individuals have of the perceptions, judgements, opinions, behaviours, etc., of other individuals (or groups).

The most general experimental paradigm for the study of these transformations consists of three phases. In the first phase, measures are obtained from a sample of subjects concerning a stimulus (more or less complex). Next, the subjects are exposed to some influence (potential influence) which can be introduced in various ways: direct interaction with one or several others, listening to a recording, reading a text (we have used this last method in our research); it is at this point in the procedure that the independent variables are most often manipulated—by varying the nature of the source, the interaction either inter-individual or symbolic, or the "message" thus communicated to the subjects. The third and last phase consists in taking a second series of measures, similar if not identical to those obtained in the first phase. It is the changes observed between the two sets of measures that are taken as the index of influence exerted in a given situation.

The theme of social influence, thus defined, has been one of the major areas of interest in social psychology: it is even one of the subjects of study considered most "proper" to the discipline. As a consequence, we have numerous explanations of such phenomena (see for a more extensive review Mugny and Doise, 1979; Doise, 1982). What types of explanation are they, and what are the conceptions of social psychology that they reveal?

3. Levels of analysis and articulation in social psychology

Doise (1978b) has shown that the same phenomenon can attract explanations on different levels. Four levels are distinguished. At the first level, explanations are sought in processes in the individual (such as "affects" and information-processing). At the second level (apparently the most "legitimate" for social psychology proper) explanations are sought uniquely in terms of the "immediate" relations between two or more individuals; this conception of social psychology is that of the psychology of small groups. These two levels, particularly the first, have certainly been the preserve of "traditionalist" social psychologists, as Doise (1978b, 51) points out:

> Very many experimental studies in social psychology have certainly originated from this level of analysis. Further, many authors have firmly asserted that the proper study of experimental social psychology is the change in individual behaviour brought about by the presence of, or interaction with, other people. This conception seems to us too narrow. A true social-psychological approach cannot afford to ignore the fact that all social interactions occur among individuals who occupy determined positions within a social context. This broader social context extends far beyond the specific situation studied by the experimenter, even while being part of it.

It is without doubt because explanation has been confined to these two levels, and continues to be so confined, that social psychology has been criticized. However, other levels of explanation can be envisaged, and indeed have been, even if to a much lesser degree.

Thus a third level bases explanation on the social position occupied by the individual(s) whose behaviours are being studied. The "subjects" are in a sense re-inserted into the relationships existing among the social groups and the social categories to which they belong or do not belong (Doise, 1978a; Tajfel, 1978). Finally, the fourth level of explanation considers the norms of behaviour which are most general in a society, and therefore most general also with regard to the dominant ideology at that particular time in its history. Until now, these latter two levels have been the poor relations of social psychology. Yet the most recent developments in the discipline have attempted to re-insert the *social* into social psychology, to integrate the processes which are studied into a more historical perspective (the "more" indicating that very much remains to be done).

Social psychology of the traditional kind has, then, limited itself to the first two levels of explanation, for which the criticism of supporting the status quo is well deserved. In being blind to the historical divisions within society, has it not behaved exactly like an ideology whose function is to mask those divisions?

A new definition of social psychology must remedy this fault. It should also be made clear that this is not merely a matter of eschewing this or that explanation: it is necessary to examine all possible levels of explanation, and in particular to attempt to integrate or, in the terminology of Doise, to "articulate" them. By articulating all the various levels of explanation involved in the study of a phenomenon, we give ourselves the theoretical means of grasping the complex processes through which individuals and groups participate in the social dynamic. We can begin to understand how the individual is integrated into society, as well as differentiated from it and acting upon it.

In this book we are particularly concerned with social influence, so let us look first at the explanations which have been offered of this. We will also look at the levels of explanation which have been neglected, and how these could be articulated into a properly social psychological explanation. This will be the first illustration of the new approach we are proposing.

4. Levels of analysis of social influence

At the first level, then, social psychologists seek explanations in processes occurring in the individual. Essentially, they are interested in the cognitive mechanisms which come into play in typical situations of social influence. The individual is seen as an information-processing organism, and the task of social psychology is to discover the rules or principles underlying these processes and, better still, to formalize them. The work of Flament (1959a,b) is typical of this type of explanation, which looks at the statistical operations applied by interacting subjects to the various responses available to them. If their responses converge, they are seen as having established a distribution of responses, abstracted its central tendency, and also a mean deviation beyond which responses are not acceptably appropriate (de Montmollin, 1977). Of this type also are theories of differential social psychology (Crutchfield, 1955, to cite but one) which explain social influence in terms of the personality traits of the individuals concerned and which lead to typologies (of individuals and situations) from which it is possible to predict who will be influenced and when. Here also, the basic mechanism of social influence is clearly located at the level of the individual.

A second type of explanation seeks the cause of social influence in the process of social interaction itself. Thus, convergence and conformity are linked to the nature of the negotiations which take place among social actors. But these negotiations are seen as taking place among individuals and groups whose relations are themselves defined only in terms of the existing social influence relations. Thus sociometric status plays an essential part: individuals who are more attractive (who are preferred) exert more influence than those who are less attractive. Similarly, the strength of inter-individual relations is seen as determining: influence is easier the more highly cohesive the group. The most commonly treated themes are, in fact, interpersonal attraction, group cohesion, sociometric status, dependence, social support, and identification, all themes which specify an immediate relationship between individuals whose affiliations beyond the influence situation are ignored.

The following is an exaggerated example concerning the definition of deviance. Freedman and Doob (1968) proposed a "psychology of being different". The subjects took a series of tests. They were then shown a truncated distribution of the results in which it appeared that they themselves were very removed from the centre of the distribution and therefore "deviant". It is important to note that these subjects did not even know the meaning of the parameters of this distribution, beyond the one fact that they themselves were deviant. Thus, deviance is defined in terms of relationship with others, even non-identified others, and with no reference to the social meaning of such deviance. This is certainly a very narrow definition of deviance.

Also interesting is the definition of the terms majority/minority within such a conception, for which we need to recall briefly the work of Asch (1951, 1956). The subject's task in these experiments was to state of which of three vertical lines of different length was equal to a standard line. The subject responded after several other people had already responded. These others were confederates of the experimenter and responded in a totally erroneous manner (there being in fact no doubt as to which was the correct response). About 30% of the subjects' responses were modified, or influenced. What kind of influence was this? Classically, there would be no doubt about it—this was majority influence, since the single subject was outnumbered by the confederates. This signifies that majority and minority are defined uniquely in terms of the parties in the immediate social interaction. We should say at once that we define these two words not in terms of immediate inter-individual relations, particularly numerical ones (though we acknowledge the significance and impact of these in influence situations), but in terms of the responses which are dominant or not dominant in a social system at a specific moment in history. Thus, even if few people responded differently from Asch's experimental subject, they would not be called a majority, but a minority, since they would be defending a position in regard to which there is no doubt whatsoever that it is non-dominant in the social milieu to which the subjects belong. (It should be noted here that the important point about the response is not that it is incorrect—so many majorities are incorrect—but that it is not dominant.) It is impossible not to assent to this interpretation, which was put forward by Moscovici in 1976.

At first sight, it would indeed seem that the processes of social influence occur at the interface of the first two levels of analysis, since changes *within* the individual are related to interactions *between* individuals. In any case, research in this field has confined itself almost entirely to these two levels. The two other levels have barely been touched directly by social psychologists, even if they are sometimes implicit in a conception relevant to the first two levels, and as far as we are aware the classic theory of social influence makes no attempt to integrate the levels.

The third level is concerned with the social positions occupied by the individuals or groups studied, and allusions to this level are not lacking, for all that it has never been conceptualized as such. Thus for example Sherif and Sherif (1969) report the work of Sampson, carried out in a monastery, which showed how reciprocal influences in a so-called normalization situation (a study of social convergence using the autokinetic effect,* Sherif, 1935) were dramatically modified by the insertion of the paradigm into a milieu characterized by conflicts among agents in different positions within the monastic institution. While the young novices converged, there was asymmetrical influence between young and "old" novices; refusals and negative responses of some kind or another even appeared when a novice and a monk were placed in this situation who differed in their ideological preferences, rather than simply in their positions within the situation.

---

* This autokinetic effect forms part of several of the studies we shall refer to, so it is worth describing it briefly here. A subject is blindfolded and brought into a room which is completely blacked out. The subject therefore has no means of self-orientation in space. A small point of light is then revealed for about two seconds. The subject's task is to estimate the amplitude of apparent movement which will be perceived

Similarly, Lemaine, Lasch and Ricateau (1971–2) have shown a link between perceptual divergences and ideological orientations, namely a dissimilation effect, whereby individuals seek to appear different from each other by modifying their responses if it becomes evident that they are similar to those of others. This effect appears in perceptual responses when the subjects involved are affiliated to rival ideologies, such as feminism versus anti-feminism.

It frequently happens, however, that researchers whose theories are grounded in the first two levels make implicit use of the third level as a source of variables which are essential to their experimental demonstrations. They fail to recognize this, since they do not follow through the theoretical implications. We have pointed out elsewhere (Mugny and Doise, 1979) such slippages between methodology and conceptualization in this very area of social influence (in particular in the case of Kelman's famous study of 1958 on the different influence processes).

Explanations at the fourth level would include factors representing ideology, which we define for our purposes as an ensemble of representations and general values acknowledged as universal within a given social system, over and above any particular social positions or categorial affiliations. Analyses at this level in the area of social influence are virtually non-existent, although several writers have been interested in changes relative to social judgements. Let us therefore try to sketch out some possible approaches to the analysis of ideological effects. At the same time, we should be able to see more exactly how this level articulates with interpretations at the other levels.

How—and above all—why do individuals converge in their responses in paradigms such as Sherif's? Why is it that individuals who have already, independently, established a stable response to the autokinetic effect converge when they are grouped together in twos or threes? We have already seen how Flament and Montmollin

---

(illusorily). Over a long series of trials, subjects always reduce the variation in their responses around a central value: in other words, they establish a subjective frame of reference for these novel judgements, setting up an individual norm in a situation which allows no objective assessment whatsoever. If several individuals, previously unknown to each other, are now placed together in this situation and asked to respond in turn, the well-replicated result is that the members of groups thus formed will establish a common norm by acknowledging a central value (not necessarily a mean value, though sometimes approaching it) and a limit of variation around this value. This is the classic paradigm for the study of social convergence.

explained this in terms of statistical operations carried out by the subjects on responses already existing within the psychosocial field, i.e.
their own and the others' responses. Other writers, such as French
(1956) or Moscovici and Ricateau (1972) see it from the point of view
of inter-individual negotiations: the convergence is the outcome of
reciprocal concessions, perhaps expressing the desire to avoid conflict
with the others. French has indeed shown that this effect holds well for
individuals of equivalent status, amongst whom a reciprocal negotiation is facilitated. Sampson, and Lemaine and his collaborators, have
further shown how the convergence is broken when the relative social
standing of individuals is made conspicuous. One question remains,
however, and it is a question which underlines the failure of these various accounts to be exhaustive: why do individuals of the same status,
in a situation in which social status is not rendered conspicuous, make
use of certain statistical procedures in order to bring about reciprocal
concessions and so avoid conflict? The type of explanation offered is
valid in itself, and also relevant. Yet no single explanation can embr-
ace the totality of this phenomenon. What is missing here is a level of
explanation which can take account of ideology. It should be realized
that the subjects in such experiments do in fact share a particular
social position: that of being subjects in a psychological experiment.
They are in a situation in which they are dominated by the experimenter, who is a representative, an agent of the institution "science".
This relationship (relevant at the third level of explanation) fore-
grounds what might be called epistemo-ideology. The subjects are
aware that they are in a university institution, one which is still largely
responsible for disseminating positivist criteria of truth, which are
founded upon regularity and inter-individual consensus. For these subjects, the verification of the psychological theory which they suspect
the experimenter of holding consists in their converging towards a
consensual response. It is to verify this theory, as a function of this
epistemo-ideology, that subjects converge, thus avoiding disagreement (which would be contrary to scientific truth) through the appli-
cation of statistical operations which allow them to estimate which
response is most likely to satisfy the verification requirement. Sperling
(1946, in Asch, 1952) has reported that even if subjects are warned
that the auto-kinetic effect is an illusion (and therefore no consensus
based on "truth" can occur) 40% of subjects still converge . . .

Other ideological notions certainly enter into the processes of social influence. We shall see plenty of detailed illustrations of this in relation to our theory of minority influence. One in particular, which has not been seriously contested, is worth pointing out here: the notion of freedom of opinion, which is one of the most general and fundamental to the way in which our society is organized. Thus, the idea of reactance phenomena (or the maintenance of autonomy which has been threatened by a human agent), although it has given rise to a theory of intraindividual motivation (Brehm, 1966) does not in the last analysis appear able to do more than indicate the involvement of ideological representations in specific experimental situations. Heilman (1976) for instance was able to show (though not within a theoretical perspective which made explicit the ideological character of the processes implied) that the principle of freedom of opinion is only effectual when the power relationship between the source of threat and the subject is concealed, and that the subject no longer acts according to this principle after the power relationship has been made explicit. Ideology, as is proper to its function, masks the fact that liberty of choice is nothing but an illusion of autonomy.

This short discussion of the social psychology of social influence plainly reveals that an articulation of explanations at several levels is more exhaustive than analysis in terms of a single level of explanation. We shall see this emerge again and again throughout this book: minority behaviours entail specific perceptions of the minority source and message which are interwoven with a specific inter-individual relationship whose meanings derive from collective representations and/or ideological aspects of the relations between dominant and dominated groups.

It is important to note that in the psychosociological analysis which we envisage no single level of analysis is preferred above any other. Unless this were the case, we would fall into "psychologism", or "social psychologism", or "sociologism", or some other variant of what could appear as a species of reductionism. Of course it is commonplace to state that there would be no society without individuals, and that there are no individuals without social attachments. Even so, the separation of disciplines leads to the creation of individuals totally abstracted from History, and to an image of society without people. And social psychologists, from whom we could have expected the needed psychosociological articulation, have been (and still appear to be) constricted within explanations in terms of inter-individual relations, if not purely individual psychology. This is why we need a new social psychology which is willing to break with such a scientific tradition.

1

How is minority influence possible?

A double sense is given to this question. In the first place, we are interested in the development of work on social influence: for decades, researchers have failed to envisage the possibility that minorities can be influential. What is the reason for this and what theoretical presuppositions have led to it? More important, what new theoretical postulates will be necessary before minority influence can become a theoretical possibility?

Once the theoretical prerequisites for a theory of minority influence have been identified, we can proceed directly to the second meaning of the question, which is: how, by what mechanisms, do minorities, in spite of the handicap of their deviance, ever manage to act within society, convert people to their cause, and insert their goals into the history of a society?

1. The "functionalist" model

In his book on social influence and social change Moscovici (1976) exposed the implicit model underlying theories of social influence, and in fact most of social psychology. This model accepts social systems as given realities (absence of historical perspective) and as optimal (non-critical integration of researchers within such systems). As a result, the criteria of normality and of deviance are treated as absolutes, the first seen as functional and adaptive and the second as dysfunctional. The place of social influence processes within such a model is easily imagined: they are seen as mechanisms of social control, ensuring social interactions which are stable, consensual, and in conformity with social norms. Hence the exclusive concentration of research arising out of this model on the process of socialization (process of normalization) and reduction of deviance (pressure toward social conformity). Ironically, the very processes studied arise out of power relations, while these power relations themselves are theoretically obscured in so far as they are taken for granted. In fact, they are never conceptualized in and for themselves. All explanations are couched in terms of direct inter-individual relationships, while the independent variables, in supposing a relationship of dependency between the target and the source, always imply that the one is ascendant over the other, and ascendant in terms of characteristics of the source which are antecedent (and therefore extraneous) to direct encounters.

Dependency, in fact, expresses a difference on a scale of social status, whether this be competence, authority, sociometric status, or numerical, etc. Thus it is always the individual or group which is higher on this scale of status which can theoretically influence the inferior individual or group. The asymmetry of status leads to an asymmetry of influence. The outcome of interactions therefore appears as a "logical" ("deduced") consequence of the difference between social actors. There is an almost exact homology between the social status relations existing in the society and the inter-individual relations of influence in the laboratory. In other words, influence is nothing more than power relations under a different guise.

It is clear, then, that within the type of theoretical framework we have so briefly discussed (with all that implies with regard to over-simplification), a theory of minority influence of the kind we envisage would be seen as neither possible (since influence is reduced to the exercise of power) nor for that matter as necessary (since the attested function of social influence is social control within an optimal, stable, social system, and not to be the driving force of innovation).

The problem of social change can nevertheless be treated without too many difficulties or modifications by the holders of this model. Consider, for example, the work of Hollander (1960, 1977), in which he proposes a theory of "idiosyncratic credit" (or of "particularism"), which divides social innovation into two phases. During the first phase, the future innovator must conform scrupulously to the norms in force within his group, an activity which will allow him to accumulate sufficient personal "credits" to assure him the status of leader. The size of his stock of credits will, in the second phase, determine whether he will be allowed to innovate (and therefore to modify certain of the group norms in force) without having to lose his status. Innovation would thus be possible, even within the functionalist model. But this is innovation from above, which, because of the social status of its originators, is reducible to a "state reformism" and implies no fundamental change in the social system.

It is precisely the question of the diffusion of innovations coming from opposed minorities which we want to examine in this book. Only a complete reversal of perspective can permit the theoretical integration of minority influence processes within a general model of social influence. Moscovici's "genetic" (or interactionist) model offers such a reversal.

2. The "genetic" model

In the genetic model, social systems no longer constitute absolute givens, but instead result from the confrontation of and negotiation among various social agents. Interactions, even when marked by status asymmetries, are seen as involving a reciprocity which assures that each agent can have a potential effect on the system. The apparent stability of a system represents only one moment out of a continual process of social change, creation, and reduction of divergences. The norms which define responses as normal or deviant are not "givens", but rather the outcome of negotiations between individuals and groups. Deviance, in this model, loses its negative character and becomes adaptive when it is innovative. The function of social influence is not reduced to that of social control but extends to processes of innovation, in so far as the maintenance of the social system is a matter of its transformation rather than its immobility. Not only does the diffusion of minority innovation become possible with such a conception, but it becomes a theoretical necessity, and those workers who have adopted this model have concentrated on such processes.

The diffusion of a minority innovation, even if it occurs within a context characterized by asymmetries of social status, is not reduced to the mere exercise of power. The variables identified are not those of dependence but those relevant to negotiation between social agents. The processes of social influence are no longer seen as the necessary result of a more or less complex arrangement of status relations whose source is held to be in relations antecedent to the interaction, but the possible result of the behaviours of persons during the interaction itself. Even if denuded of power, a social entity can nevertheless theoretically exert influence. Let us see how.

scovici's theory of consistency

If the influence exerted by a minority source does not derive from a power relationship, because such a relationship would always be unfavourable to it, where does it derive from? At this level, the reversal of perspective proposed by Moscovici (1976) is complete: the source of minority influence lies in the meanings which arise out of the set of minority behaviours at the time of encounters, and from the negotiations between minority source and potential receivers. It is important to stress that the crucial meanings do not lie in the nature of alternative contents, but in the organization, or structure, of these contents. This being the case, we have a theoretical notion whose role is decisive: that of behavioural style.

For Moscovici (1976, pp. 110, 111, 112):

> Behavioural style is a novel, and yet familiar, concept. It refers to the organization of behaviours and opinions, and the timing and intensity of their expression—in short, it refers to the "rhetoric" of behaviour and opinion. Behaviours *per se*, like the individual sounds of a language, have no meaning of their own. Only in combination, as determined by the individual or group, and as interpreted by those to whom they are addressed, can they have meaning and arouse reaction.

> The person or group who adopts one of these styles must, if the style is to be socially recognized and identified, meet the following three conditions:
> (a) be aware of the relationship between their internal state and the external signals they are using. Certainty is manifested by an affirmative, confident tone; for example, the intention not to make any concessions is expressed by consistency of the appropriate behaviour;
> (b) use signals systematically and consistently, so as to prevent misunderstanding on the part of the receiver;
> (c) preserve the same relationships between behaviours and meanings throughout an interaction—in other words, ensure that words do not change their meaning during the course of an interaction.

> In social interaction, these conventional ways of organizing behaviour are meant to give the other group or person information about the position and motivation of the person or group initiating the interaction.

It is therefore by means of the consistency of its style of behaviour that a minority can become influential. Consistency is distinguishable from an inconsistent style of behaviour according to several parameters:

> from the *diachronic*, or historical, point of view consistency is characterized by the firm, systematic, and non-contradictory repetition of the same mode of response;

from the *synchronic*, or contemporary, point of view consistency is characterized by the existence of an intraminority consensus, that is, a total unanimity among minority members regarding the expression of minority positions.

By means of such consistency, the minority transmit information not only about their own definition of a particular stimulus or specific reality, but also about themselves. In this way, the minority emphasizes its commitment to a particular position and at the same time signals its firmness in the face of any test. Such self-confidence assures it of an important capacity for auto-reinforcement; whoever joins the minority can expect to find social support within a durable consensus. The minority can also revalue itself as an alternative through the example of personal sacrifices, which must sometimes be made (responding to reprisals, ridicule, incomprehension).

Through its consistency, the minority also demonstrates its self-motivation and its ability to act outside the worn grooves of conformity. It is a model of autonomy, able to lead receivers of its message to re-affirm (and perhaps even recover) their own.

Consistency, then, is characterized by behaviours which are defended with firmness and constancy over time and across different situations. Since this is such an important notion for the development of our argument, we shall report briefly here on how the first illustrative experiments went about operationalizing minority consistency.

4. Operationalizations of consistency

In an early experiment (Faucheux and Moscovici, 1967) subjects were shown geometric designs varying on several dimensions such as size, colour, etc. Subjects had to decide which dimension they preferred (the task being presented as deciding which dimensions would be most rapidly and effectively discriminable to aid decision-making in aircraft navigation). A confederate of the experimenter, placed in groups of four or five subjects, always (on 64 trials) made the same response, namely "colour". The results showed an increase in the number of "colour" responses by the other subjects.

Another example is an experiment carried out by Moscovici, Lage and Naffrechoux (1969) which has already become a standard paradigm. The subjects were asked to give a simple colour name to

the colour (blue) projected by a slide. In some of the experimental
conditions, the subjects (of whom there were four) were accompanied
by two confederates who responded in accordance with a pre-
arranged programme which ensured that their responses were virtually totally incorrect. In some groups, they responded "green" to all
items (consistency condition); in others they only gave this response
two-thirds of the time (inconsistency condition). As predicted by consistency theory, minority influence (about 8%) was greater when the
confederates' responses were invariant. The consistent repetition of
the same response can, therefore, be a source of minority influence.
   It should also be pointed out that these authors showed a further
minority influence effect, this time on responses which were less
directly under conscious control. Following the conflict interaction
described above, the subjects were given a test of colour discrimination. It was found that there was a tendency to classify more colour
samples as green than was the case following conditions in which
minority influence had not occurred. Such delayed effects are very
important and have been confirmed using more subtle measures (such
as the chromatic after-effect: Moscovici and Personnaz, 1980; Doms,
1978; Doms and Van Avermaet, 1980a). In view of the complexity of
this question, we shall not pursue it further in this chapter, except to
point out that it is often difficult for a subject to acknowledge minority
influence openly and publicly.
   The two experiments described illustrate the impact of minority
consistency as defined diachronically, i.e. taking place over time. The
idea of synchronic, or contemporaneous consistency has not been
examined experimentally. This idea emerges from a reinterpretation
of experiments using a paradigm similar to that used by Asch. This
paradigm was reinterpreted by Moscovici as one showing typical
minority influence. Therefore Asch (1951) himself studied the effect of
intra-minority coherence and showed that if one of the members of a
minority abandons it and begins to give non-consensual responses, the
influence of the minority is considerably diminished and may even
cease altogether.
   Allen (1975) has elaborated a paradigm for the study of this question. Still viewing Asch's experiments within the tradition of majority
influence, Allen was interested in the social support available for nonconformity. For him the question was: to what extent does a weakening of majority consensus allow the experimental subject (whether

minority or deviant!) to escape from majority pressure? There are several experiments which could answer this question as well as the question posed by Moscovici (reinterpreting this paradigm in the same way as Asch's): to what extent does a weakening of minority consensus allow the experimental subject (one of the majority) to escape from minority consistency? One of the plainest answers to this question is that any failure of synchronic consistency as defined by intra-minority consensus would imply a failure of minority influence. But such an answer rests on a number of re-interpretations, with all the dangers entailed by that. For the moment, however, let us accept that the idea of synchronic consistency is a theoretically valid one, and ask a further question about the nature of domains of innovation.

It would be reasonable to expect that consistency would be more easily defined in the perceptual domain, where, more than anywhere else, naïve responses appear to be the expression of epistemological consistency. Nevertheless, there are several examples demonstrating that consistency is easily operationalized in the field of social judgements also, whether by the repetition of positions and arguments (Nemeth and Wachtler, 1973; Paicheler, 1976, 1977) or by the degree of coherence in argumentation (Mugny, 1975). The latter experiment was carried out at a time when a referendum was being held about the employment of foreigners for casual labour in Switzerland. The experiment took place in a canton which had a tradition of favourable attitudes toward foreigners. Two types of text were distributed. One took a very unfavourable (xenophobic) position toward "guest workers" and would have denied them residential, economic, political, and trade union rights. The other text was strongly favourable toward guest workers (anti-xenophobic), and would have afforded equal rights to all workers. Within each type of text, there were consistent and inconsistent variables (which were perceived as such, according to *ad hoc* measures we took). Consistency was defined by the repetition of the same position in relation to different problems (favourable or unfavourable to residential, economic, political, and trade union rights) and by the conviction of the statements of position. All other features of the text being equated, inconsistency was expressed through hesitation in affirming or denying, contradictions between statements in the text, and ambiguity in the proposed solutions. Measures of attitude change between a pre- and post-questionnaire showed positive effects of the consistent texts only, and of both types of text (xenophobic and anti-xenophobic). Furthermore, the anti-xenophobic text was the more influential, demonstrating the importance, over and above consistency, of the nature of the minority norm itself.

We do not intend to go into further detail here concerning the various forms which consistency can take (for this, see Moscovici's book); suffice it to say that diachronic consistency is characterized by coherence, repetition, firmness, confidence, and the expression of autonomy, while synchronic consistency is defined as intra-minority consensus. What is more important here is the question of why consistency is such an important source of minority influence.

5. Consistency and social conflict

By definition, a minority position is defined by the difference between its behaviours, judgements, etc. and those dictated by the dominant norms. However, difference alone does not imply the possibility of, nor the seeking after, influence. In many cases, difference is an expression of withdrawal or deviance (Merton, 1957)—in short, of anomie. It is consistency *within* difference which allows the active minority to define itself in the history of the social system of which it forms part. By virtue of its consistency, its difference becomes a coherent alternative model, existing alongside the dominant model yet counter to its norms.

By virtue of its consistency, the minority possesses an essential power also: that of setting up an apparently insoluble social problem, since it is in the very negotiations which constitute social exchange that the consistent minority refuses to compromise. Its strength lies in blocking negotiation with the representatives of the dominant model. Social instability is therefore created by constantly drawing attention to the fallibility of the dominant model. The minority creates uncertainty, and furthermore a type of uncertainty which can be resolved by adopting or at least moving toward the alternative norms proposed.

The instability created has two aspects. Firstly, the minority breaks the social contract, the rules of the game according to which the minority must conform to the majority. The minority therefore becomes a model of dissidence. Several experimental studies (Tuddenham, 1961; Maier and McRay, 1972; Kimball and Hollander, 1974) have shown how the minority can lead subjects to respond in an independent manner, independent of the minority as well as of the majority. Consistency may also be important as a social support for nonconformity (Allen, 1975) in historical contexts where latent social tensions are leading to the emergence of new orientations. Secondly, the focussing of attention on the minority and its conspicuous consistency means that dominant behaviours cannot remain unchanged; either they must be reinforced in order to reject the alternatives proposed by the minority or they must be modified in order to approach closer to them. This is an essential point: the consistency of minority behaviours ensures (or can ensure) the recognition of the content of minority positions.

Nevertheless, we should not expect miracles (as is sometimes done in the experimental approach to these phenomena). It is obvious that the minority does not bring about instant acquiescence on the part of everyone. Social change takes place in a context of tensions, where the dominant norms are supported by power and its apparatus (ideological as well as repressive). Furthermore, experiments show that influence is reluctantly acknowledged in subjects' overt or social responses, and is more often manifested indirectly and in extremely subtle ways. This is a point to which we shall often return.

Now that we have outlined the main points of the consistency theory let us consider some possible developments of the theory.

6. Pending questions

The first point to note is that although we have focused thus far on styles of behaviour, and on effective minority behaviours, it is not possible to study these without taking into acount the way in which they appear to, or are represented to themselves by, the populations concerned. Moscovici showed himself aware of this aspect in making systematic use of post-experimental measures designed to capture the effects of consistency at the level of subjects' representation of the source. It is often at this level that the criteria which define consistency are manifest: involvement in interaction, independent judgement, firmness, courage . . .

Consistency as operationally defined may have several different appearances at this level of representation, which will depend on how situations are designed by the experimenter. Thus, for example, in order to be recognized as such, consistency might have to be manifested as a clear expression of independent decision. This was the case in an experiment by Nemeth and Wachtler (1974) in which a confederate in a simulated jury defended an unpopular position. There were two experimental conditions. In one, the confederate was seen to deliberately select a seat at the head of a rectangular table—a position which is known to facilitate the influence of whoever occupies it (Strodbeck and Hook, 1961). In the other condition, the confederate was instructed to take the same seat by the experimenter. It was only when the confederate had been seen to select the seat himself that his influence was greater in this position. He had given evidence of autonomy and confidence.

In a somewhat similar manner, the operationalization of consistency can appear as rigidity or lack of flexibility to receivers, in situations where minority behaviours do not appear to adapt themselves to systematic changes. Consistency does not necessarily entail invariance of response. Nemeth *et al.* (1974) used the same paradigm we have just described, and introduced a variation using a series of blue slides varying in illumination intensity. In the experimental conditions, the confederates either responded incorrectly "green" to all the stimuli or "green" to slides of one intensity and "blue-green" to the others. Their influence was greatest in the latter condition, in which their responses varied as a function of variations in the stimuli. When they did not vary their response, their influence was very slight. It is possible that the subjects doubted the discriminative abilities of the minority source, and therefore attributed their responses to rigidity.

Consistency, therefore, can not only undergo various operationalizations, but different styles of consistency can each take on varying significance according to particular situations. We merely note here the importance of cognitive representations of minority behaviours (as opposed to their consistency *per se*), which can be modulated by the situation. Nevertheless, this book is seeking a theorization of these representations which will be valid across situations, in the manner pioneered by Moscovici.

After the question of representations, a second point requiring discussion is the relevance of Kelley's (1967) attribution theory. According to this theory, a behaviour (or a set of behaviours) is imputed to an internal cause, to an object, or to a person when the effect (here, behaviours) is tied to this person, when the behaviours are stable across time and across situations and when there is consensus among persons. Diachronic and synchronic consistency are indeed notions which appear to be coterminous with Kelley's concept of attribution (Moscovici, 1972). The norms proposed by a consistent minority would, therefore, be validated by this process of stable attribution. The difficulty is that Kelley's model presupposes that persons are rational: they carry out a sort of analysis of variance from which they deduce the probability that a particular proposed reality is plausible (here, the minority model). This model has already been criticized (Apfelbaum and Herzlich, 1970–1971; Deschamps, 1977) essentially because it fails to include certain factors which cut across the apparent rationality of attributions. These factors reside in the relationships between social positions and ideological representations. The important question, therefore, is the following: when will consistent behaviour be perceived as the symbolic reflection ("correct") of *reality*, and when will it be perceived as the consequence of *bias*, either intrinsic to the minority itself, or imposed by external conditions? Alternatively, following Kelley's model, while it is possible to state the conditions of the attribution of stable characteristics to a minority, it is not possible to infer from these whether the stable properties will be in turn attributed to the environment or to minority bias. As we shall see, representations of a different order intervene, which have their origin in the dominant normative system itself, and particularly those concerning the relationship between majority and minorities.

The third point in this section is more methodological and concerns the use of perceptual tasks for the demonstration of the causes of minority influence. There is a contradiction between theoretical statements and experimental realizations: Moscovici defines a source as a minority in so far as it is in conflict with a dominant normative system, and in so doing he rejects a numerical characterization of minority status (a position which has incidentally led him to reinterpret the Asch effect as a minority effect). Nevertheless, in the experiments he has carried out, majority and minority are once more distinguished in numerical terms. Could this be a minority strategy—is not his model just such?—to hoist the dominant majority with its own petard? Whatever we say about this problem, although we must take note of it, it does not invalidate the theory itself, nor the general model. A more serious consequence attaches to the use of perceptual materials, at least for those who, like us, believe that there is a real "dialectic" between theory and experiment. Hypotheses must be open to continual modification. Since, within a culture, at least, subjects most often agree in their perceptual judgements independently of whatever social positions they may occupy, the use of perceptual materials in experiments largely masks the complexity of the social context of innovation. It follows that experimental hypotheses will not be open to change and adjustment in the light of the unexpected results which always enrich theory. In the typical experiment, we have on one side the majority, namely the subjects who respond "correctly", and on the other side a minority, the confederates who respond erroneously. *What is being studied therefore are majority/minority relations removed from the context of social power** in which minorities are truly enmeshed, yet the study hopes to establish the model of functioning of the minority. We have shown elsewhere (Mugny, 1975) that the use of social judgements already existing in a "real-life" situation of social tension (the army, xenophobia pollution) allows us to reason from the starting-point of majority/minority relations within a social power context. Thus we have the paradoxical situation that the functionalist approach to social influence does not rest on an explicit theory of power, yet identifies variables at this level, since dependency always expresses a power relationship, while the genetic model, which is aware of such

---

* The use of perceptual paradigms, with no reference to the power relations characteristic of the social context of innovation, might well explain the difficulties which sometimes arise in distinguishing between majority and minority influence. The numerical criterion in fact defines majorities and minorities who are really, *normatively, both minorities*. Whether there are two or four people stating that a blue slide is green matters less than the fact that they are a minority in terms of habitual norms of judgement. Thus it is possible for the meanings of "majority" and "minority" to vary. It is even possible to conceptualize *minority* pressure as increasing with the number (numerical majority) of confederates defending this position. This is indeed how we would re-interpret some results obtained by Doms (1978) which appear to be in conflict with Moscovici's theory. These results showed that the influence of a numerical majority was equal (at the time of a second post-test) to that of a (numerical) minority, on a measure of indirect effects. But the minority pressure, defined in terms of norms, could well have been stronger for *numerical* reasons, and thus have delayed the appearance of the indirect effect which is the usual sign of minority influence. This state of affairs is explained by the absence of any systematic knowledge on our part of the mental representations evoked by the notions of majority and minority in domains where social norms can privilege, or handicap, original positions. This is another area urgently needing research.

relationships (to the point that it distinguishes them from influence relationships), makes use of experiments which obscure the existence of these very relationships. Our view is that this is an outcome of the choice of method. This choice may also explain, incidentally, the relationship of the theory of consistency to Kelley's (1967) attribution model, one of the difficulties of which is precisely in accounting for the effects of power in the inferential processes it analyses.

The last problem is not in itself the most important but it is useful to point out that it affects our own earliest studies on minority influence (Mugny, 1974). These studies attempted to deal with an apparent contradiction between the theory of consistency as a source of minority influence, and some conflicting experimental results. Schachter's (1951) experiment, for instance, was among the first studies of minority influence, in his case looking at the effects of various types of deviants within groups. Confederates instructed to act according to principles laid down by the experimenter were placed in discussion groups. Thus one of them would at first be very distant from the group's positions, but subsequently approach so closely to them as to adopt them. Another deviant would remain stable at the position initially taken by the preceding deviant, thus conforming well to the definition of consistency put forward by Moscovici. However, after half an hour of discussion, signs of rejection of this deviant began to appear; in particular, communications which would formerly have been addressed to him now begin not to be, and in an allocation of roles to be taken up later in the discussion, he was given a subordinate position.

Moscovici himself, with Doise (1969–70) has demonstrated the risks of minority consistency. Subjects were asked to characterize as introvert or extravert the behaviour of a student described in a booklet. In a control condition, subjects responded in pairs about the same booklet. In the experimental conditions, three persons were involved. The third was said to be present in a neighbouring room where the experimenter went to collect their response (in fact simulated). In the booklet, the student's behaviour was at first described as clearly introverted, then becoming gradually clearly extraverted. In some groups, the experimenter attributed a consistent "introvert" response to the simulated subject; in this case the deviance only appeared gradually, or was delayed. In other groups the simulated response was consistently "extravert", and the deviance was thus immediate and abrupt.

The overall result of this experiment (which was more complex than we have described) was that the gradual or delayed deviancy had some influence (the subjects gave more "introvert" responses), but the immediately deviant responses were rejected, as was indicated by an increased number of "introvert" responses by the subjects.

There would therefore seem to be a contradiction between the consistency theory of minority influence and the empirical finding that even a consistent minority can bring about a "boomerang" effect.

These four pending questions—the relation between minority behaviours and their cognitive representation in various situations, the association between consistency theory and an unsatisfactory theory of attribution, the use of perceptual tasks, in which power relations are less apparent, and finally the discrepancy between theory and empirical findings—have led us to propose a development of Moscovici's consistency theory. This will be described in the next chapter.

2

A psychosociological theory
of minority influence

In this chapter we attempt to conceptualize the psychosocial processes which act to diffuse minority innovations. The theory we propose is an extension of Moscovici's (1976) consistency theory and also over-comes certain difficulties implicit in this notion. As we emphasized in the introduction, our theory aims to articulate the different levels of analysis which are *necessary* for a complete understanding of the phenomena we are seeking to explain. We shall see from the outset that the diffusion of minority innovations takes place within a context of social change and resistance to such change. To this context must be articulated "direct" relationships (actual contact, or "symbolic", i.e. mediated by some more distant form of communication); subjects' processing of the information they receive (recognition of an alterna-tive position, image of the influence source) which may vary depend-ing on the social context of the situation, e.g. whether it is natural or experimentally induced; and finally, within this social context, the relations between groups. These latter are essential because of the ideological social representations and actions to which they give rise.

The theory will be proposed in the form of general propositions, without offering at this stage any experimental illustrations. The experiments will be described from the next chapter onwards, once the theory has been fully explained, so as to give the reader the chance to properly assess theory and experiment against each other. In real-ity, however, our conceptual advance has followed behind the development of our experimental paradigms—so much so that it is now difficult for us to say which theoretical propositions were *a priori* deductions and which were inductions from apparently negative experimental results. This is to say, we recognize the continuous dialectic between initially too general hypotheses, and experimental operationalizations which, fortunately, oblige us to modify the theory.

We move now to a point-by-point presentation of the theory.

1. The diffusion of a minority innovation takes place within a complex context of social change and resistance to this change

When individuals have to state the colour of blue slides or to say which of three lines is the same length as a standard line, and there is no ambiguity in the situation, we can legitimately expect that they will all respond correctly, if we exempt certain anomalies (of visual perception, for example). All subjects, whatever their social position or standing on the various rankings of social status (power, competence, etc.) have acquired the means of perception and coding of physical reality, means which they use without difficulty in these experimental situations. There is therefore unanimity without conflict (even latent) among these individuals; they constitute a majority which is both numerical and normative. If we now introduce a confederate who gives responses in conflict with the evidence, he is easily seen as a deviant against the consensual majority. In this case we have two opposed entities: a majority and a minority. Clearly, then, inter-individual negotiations will be an essential characteristic of such situations, and the consistent "blockage" constituted by the minority's behaviour may well be the most important factor in its ability to exert social influence. In these types of situation, consistency alone may be sufficient.

This bipolar division between majority and minority is generalized by the adherents of a functionalist model to all the situations they have conceived of, even including those which involve social judgements. The majority standpoint is that which is accepted by the greatest number, that which is most "popular". It is not difficult to defend the view that such an interpretation, since it masks a power relationship, is merely an ideological conception of the term "majority". Let us then proceed to do just this, and attempt to remove the mask which has up to now prevented our full understanding of the processes we are interested in.

Suppose we study within the usual social influence paradigm, not perceptual judgements (which, as we have seen, are not affected in any obvious way by social divisions other than inter-individual disagreements brought about by the confederates) but social judgements. Consider one of our own experiments, in which the subjects judged the conservatism or progressivism of statements about the national army of Switzerland. These subjects were relatively, if obscurely, resistant to the idea of an army, which to them was a symbol of unacceptable violence. They were adolescent boys who were soon, themselves, to be obliged to do their military service, and in most cases they would in fact do it, since at the time of the study there had been a renewed clamp-down on refusals to serve (on conscientious objectors and also on movements toward democratic expression within the army). This clamp-down had been the reaction to a resurgence of strongly anti-militarist opinion, expressed particularly in the publication of a "manifesto" by 32 churchmen. At the same time, these subjects could see certain points in favour of having an army (we must, after all, defend our frontiers; military service is good character training, and there is the comradeship . . .) which led most of them to accept (reluctantly perhaps, but still to accept) military service. Their position therefore was close to (even though ostensibly in opposition) that dominant in the country as a whole, in which the army takes a large proportion of the national expenditure, and is a "popular" army in the sense that most people have actually served in it.

Even so, is it possible to speak of a *majority* viewpoint here? The answer must be "no": although there is the appearance of a consensus (and there certainly is one in the sense of a "lowest common denominator"), there are relations of dominance which cut across this majority and divide it very deeply. In fact, this apparent consensus is the result of the alienation of some people from the power held by others. Our subjects, in the course of their passage through the various ideological apparatuses of the state (family, school, work, higher education) have interiorized a dominant ideology which has been diffused by the power network from which they themselves are excluded (at this time, they do not even have the right to vote). They are also legally subject to the military institution and therefore to the risks of opposing it. These, then, are two good reasons for sharing "majority" ideas, and also two good reasons why we should distinguish, within the term majority, two social entities which are distinct precisely because they are in a clearly defined relationship: on one side there is the power which dictates norms and rules, on the other side there is the "population" (analogously with experimental terminology) which submits to domination by this power and which, through its interiorization of the dominant ideology participates wholly or partly in the norm- and rule-enforcing activities and thus becomes a "majority".

Let it be made clear at this point that a "*population*" is no more real than "public opinion" (Bourdieu, 1973). The former, sometimes also referred to as the "silent majority", should be seen as a complex fabric of sub-groups or small social categories whose relations of consent or opposition to power may vary in directness, and which may therefore vary in the extent to which they are sensitive to alternative positions, particularly those emanating from minorities. The "population sample" in our experiments have been young people aged between fifteen and twenty, not only because, their social identity being in flux, they offer greater opportunities for the experimental discovery of the subtle mechanisms of minority diffusion but also because their particular social position makes them more susceptible to certain social changes than adults, whose longer occupancy of a particular social niche may have congealed their identity or have integrated them more firmly into the dominant system.

Superimposed on this first power relationship, whose nature is both ideological and repressive, is a second series of relations with one (or more) minorities who are in frank opposition to the dominant power.

Given the complexity of these relationships, it is no more possible to carry out a theoretical analysis of minority behaviours within the framework of the unique relationship of a particular minority with a particular majority (as was the case in the perceptual experiments), since the "majority" includes several different entities, each having a different position in a power relationship.

The first difficulty is to specify which of the relations with these two entities (power and population) arises out of influence processes as such. In fact, a *choice* will have to be made.

Therefore, we will consider that minority/power relations do not arise directly out of social influence processes, but rather out of processes of confrontation, rejection and estrangement which are incompatible with any idea of exchange or "bargaining". The difference is not necessarily clear-cut; nevertheless our choice is not really arbitrary, since the processes underlying such antagonism derive directly from a particular conceptualization of power and counter-power. The strategies of minorities when confronted with power derive from their analysis of the situation and of the power relation; they are the outcome of a cost–benefit analysis. As we have seen, minorities are able, by means of their consistency, to ensure that some social conflicts are resolved in their favour and also to prevent the "co-option" of their aims, even when power is in a position to negotiate or bargain. Even so, it is surprising how many minority movements have been defused as soon as all or even only some of their demands have been met. Such examples show well enough that the minority/power relationship is not simply a matter of influence, but of power strategies: if power "co-opts" a movement, that is not to say that it has been convinced by it—the movement is defused as it is incorporated. In studying the styles of minority behaviour, particularly the flexibility or rigidity of minority influence strategies, we should not lose sight of the fact that they derive from very broad social relationships which could justify and even legitimate them. We can see already that the influence effects of rigid styles, in particular, will not be independent of the social relationships which give rise to them.

We shall postulate, then, that influence processes as such arise out of the minority/population relationship, and therefore that the population is the stake in the game of minority influence, just as this same population is the stake in the power/population dominance relationship. The minority/population relationship is the only one which does not arise directly out of the exercise of power (or of counter-power). The minority cannot use power—since this is precisely what it does not possess—to convince the population.

To grasp the processes by which one or several minorities win over a population, we need to situate them within this complex triangular relationship: power/population/minority. It is within this framework, as we shall see, that the apparent exceptions to the effectiveness of minority consistency can be explained. Minority consistency is not only such in relation to the dominant entity and its norms but also in relation to the population, which, as we have seen, is the real target of these influence processes. On the other hand, minority influence attempts bring to attention and call into question the direction in which power habitually flows, and so they induce the authorities to try to contain minority movements.

Authorities do this by instituting ideological regulations (if they do not exist already) or, if these fail, by introducing repressive regulations. The authorities enjoy power which must be retained at all costs, and their possession of this power would be called into question if one or more minorities were to expand, either diachronically (in a "war of attrition" against authority) or synchronically, by beginning to win over the population. Kiesler and Pallak (1975) have pointed out the "snowballing" effect of successful minority influence attempts.)

The complexity of the social context within which minority influence processes take place is illustrated in Fig. 1.

This diagram is subject to three qualifications before it can be used to make explicit the articulations necessary for a theory of minority influence processes:

(i) Power is understood here in a very broad sense and refers to any form of institutionalized domination.

(ii) S is used for population to avoid confusion with power, P, and also by analogy with S meaning experimental subject, because in our experiments it is the member of this "population" who make up our "experimental populations".

(iii) We defer for the present any discussion of the relations among sub-entities within a larger entity; those relevant to the theory will be considered later.

First of all, note that we distinguish theoretically at least three entities: power, population, and minority. It is important to emphasize that each one of these entities is composed of several sub-entities whose precise reference must eventually be made clear. Among the three major entities exist relationships of a very different type:

(a) between power and population, power (or any form of domination) is the essential form of relationship;

(b) between power and minority, the relationship is essentially one of antagonism;

(c) a relationship of social influence exists between minority and population.

Our theory will consist in locating the minority/population influence relationship at a point of articulation with the antagonistic relationship between power and minority, and we shall show that minority consistency arises out of this latter relationship. The minority/population relationship *per se* will be studied in terms of the negotiations between these two entities, in particular with reference to the more or less rigid styles of the minority, as well as with reference to the population's mode of perception or representation of the minority. We shall then see how these behaviours and representations take their orientation from the articulation between influence relations and power relations which criss-cross the population. A discussion of the

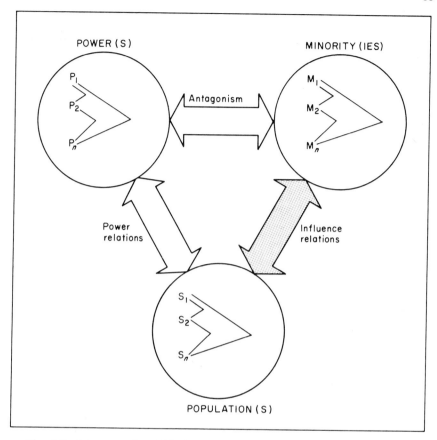

POWER (S)   MINORITY (IES)

P_1
P_2 Antagonism
P_n M_1
                                                M_2
                                                M_n

Power   Influence
relations   relations

S_1
S_2
S_n

POPULATION (S)

Fig. 1 Social context in which the diffusion of minority influence takes place

ideological, which in some manner transcends all these relationships, will complete the theoretical construction. We will show how varying interpretations can be given to the relationship of antagonism between minority and power, bringing about very different influence effects.

2. The consistency of minority behaviours defines the alternative within a relationship of antagonism

Consistency has the effect of defining the outlines of a minority's position. In order to present itself as an alternative, the minority is forced to stand in total opposition to power and therefore to break off all negotiations with it. Consistency and firmness across time and across situations are also necessary if the minority is to be perceived as an alternative: it must be seen as being different from power, yet stable. Here we can see the importance of attribution processes such as those described by Kelley (1967), since the population must be able to perceive minority consistency even while the consensus sought by power is crumbling; the population must be able to attribute to the minority a position which is always recognizable. This is one point of articulation which defines the cognitive processes by means of which the population discriminates the positions within a minority/power antagonism relationship and recognizes the precise limits of the minority position. This articulation is a constant and necessary element in the social influence process. Here we differ somewhat from Moscovici; we assert that *consistency is certainly necessary, but it is not sufficient* to account for social influence. It must be emphasized, however, that consistency is not merely a matter of the limits defining an alternative. Consistency also gives the population information about the minority itself, about its firmness, commitment, autonomy, etc., as Moscovici has clearly shown. This information, as we shall see, is essential if the recognition of a position is to be followed by approach toward that position, and thus for minority influence to take place. It is for this reason that we assert that consistency is necessary.

Before we discuss the complementary conditions of minority influence, it is important to make clear some of the consequences of our conception of consistency as an articulation of cognitive processes (i.e. the processing of information) with antagonistic social relations. This articulation can permit antagonism sometimes to take the form of the repression, by power, of minority activities, in such a way that the minority loses social visibility. Borrowing a term from Personnaz (1975/6), we may say that the minority can become *clandestinized*. It may even be forced to recant its previous position, yet still retain influence (Personnaz, 1979). In other words, minority behaviours are not simply read, they are interpreted. When subjects are able to see a minority defection as necessitated by the situation (as for instance under the threat of reprisals) they can still perceive the consistent limits of the minority position. Conversely, if a defection is not fully justified by situational constraints, it may be perceived as a lack of consistency, and may diminish the attractiveness of the minority group (cf. the experimental example given by Kiesler and Pallack, 1975). In some cases, it may even appear as a desertion or betrayal.

Consistency, then, qualifies the perception of minority behaviours in an antagonistic relationship, when the minority is in a stance of firm and coherent opposition towards power. What are the consequences of this first articulation for the influence relations proper between minority and population?

3. Consistency generates conflict not only with power, but also with population; conflict with the population must be negotiated; styles of negotiation

We shall now focus on the relationship between minority and population, while keeping clearly in view the fact that this is articulated upon the complex relationship discussed in the preceding paragraph.

The minority/population relationship is also characterized by conflict. We should recall the complexity of the social context of innovation, within which we have recognized a dominance relationship between power and population. Conflict arises out of this relationship of constraint, in fact of double constraint—it is both ideological and repressive.

We have already seen that the population partly shares the ideology diffused by the institutions of power. Given such an alienating framework, it is obvious that the population will not, at the outset, be sympathetic to the alternative position represented by the consistent minority, and they may even be hostile to it. Here, then, is a prime ideological conflict. *This conflict must be negotiated before the minority can exert influence.*

In certain conditions, and within certain limits which we shall discuss later, it is possible for a minority to negotiate with the population without this causing its opposition to power, and therefore its consistency, to be brought into question. Two types of negotiation are possible and are in fact complementary. The first type is what might be called formal; it is focussed, for instance, on questions of procedure, or "second-order" decisions. Another type of negotiation is more ideological; it consists in the consideration of compromises on ideological matters over which there are a risk of fundamental disagreement and the risk of total rejection of the minority position. In so far as our experimental illustrations are essentially (even if not unequivocally) concerned with ideological negotiations, we shall use them to provide an example. Suppose that a minority wish to convince a population that "The capitalist national army is a danger to the working class, being opposed to all forms of socialism, so we must struggle both inside and outside the army to weaken it". Suppose further that the population approves conscientious objection as a form of action against this violent institution. If, now, the minority suddenly asserts that conscientious objection is nothing but an individualist stance, and that the true struggle must be both inside and outside the army, this will exacerbate the already existing conflict between the minority's antimilitarist position and the much more finely graduated positions within the population. If the minority goes further and denounces conscientious objection as bourgeois and reactionary, the population will reject its position altogether. The diffusion of the minority norm will have failed, because of the *rigidity* of the minority's negotiation style. It can certainly be confirmed that rigidity in such a situation will obstruct minority influence, although the mechanism involved is a matter for later analysis.

Now consider, in contrast, a minority which, having asserted its judgement of conscientious objection as individualist, returns to this point to say that this can be a good method if used collectively, but that struggle both inside and outside the army is also important. This minority is more *flexible* in its relation with the population. On a point about which the population has fixed opinions which will not readily be questioned, it negotiates with delicacy, yet without sacrificing its consistency, since its stance toward power remains unchanged. This flexible minority will have more influence than a rigid one.

It should be noted that this negotiation is not only ideological: there is an undoubted formal aspect to it, in the sense that the attenuation of the ideological statement is also an attenuation of the intrasituational conflict. By ceding, the minority avoids the setting up of resistances in the population.

We are not here valuing one style of minority negotiation above the other. The effectiveness of each style depends on the minority's aims and on the particular situation. As Moscovici has pointed out, there are some situations in which one cannot but be rigid. Furthermore, the minority's aims may entail a polarization of the population: it may wish to attract only those who will be very favourable towards it and who will therefore help increase minority pressure. In certain conditions, it may be more important for the minority's cohesion, especially, for some of its actions to be unmistakably "rigid", so that only those individuals most likely to reinforce the minority position will be attracted. Thus, it should be clear that flexibility is not automatically more effective than rigidity. The effects and processes implied by different styles in different situations are more important than global quantitative evaluations.

There is a further reason why it is not possible to judge one of these behavioural styles as being overall more effective than the other: the two styles have different effects at different levels of response in the population.

4. Minority influence is not direct and instantaneous. It is latent and sometimes delayed. A rigid negotiating style accentuates this effect

Allen (1965) provided an overview of the situational variables which affect social influence. Thus, the situations set up by Asch rarely produced an influence effect which went beyond the direct relationship between subjects and confederates, in other words public influence. This is not to say that "true" influence (as Allen, and many other writers, describes these effects) does not take place: it does occur but is expressed in private situations, once outside the social constraints characteristic of the experimental phase of influence. We do not intend to discuss such effects here, nor the many operationalizations of them which are possible, but simply to make the point that there are two levels of influence directly relevant to our purpose.

Suppose that an active minority defends the positions x and x', and that it is possible to infer, from these, other responses that the minority would certainly give, say, y or w. Questionnaire items measuring opinions or judgements before and after an influence attempt (and therefore also measuring this influence) may also refer to the positions x and x'. Other questionnaire items (y or w in our example) may not have entered explicitly into the minority's utterances, yet they are clearly related to the minority's positions. Anticipating a little our experimental evidence for this, it is possible to confirm that influence is very often less in relation to the questionnaire items explicitly referred to by the minority. There are other corroborating instances of the difficulty which minorities have in influencing the "social" responses of the population. Moscovici *et al.* (1969), using a perceptual task, showed that influence on latent responses (which they related to a "perceptual code") was greater in proportion as the subjects had refused to yield overtly to the minority during the interaction phase of the experiment. Other research has found a similar phenomenon using an after-effect measure (Doms, 1978; Doms and Van Avermaet, 1980a; Moscovici, 1980; Moscovici and Personnaz, 1980; Personnaz, 1979). Yet another related phenomenon, a "sleeper effect", has been interpreted in similar terms (Moscovici *et al.*, 1981) as indicating that minority influence is not necessarily immediately observable but may appear after a time interval.

The type of effect may depend on the type of constraint which power exerts on the population, for instance, whether there is actual repression or whether repression is potential, in the form of threats.

In Western societies at the present time, power does not rely on actual repression: "ideology" is the preferred mode of constraint (Althusser, 1976). Nevertheless, the prospect of open repression is sometimes displayed towards minorities, and by extension towards those who would join or even approach them. The members of a population therefore tend to avoid explicit expression of positions which could be identified with that of a minority (later we will discuss further the origins of this avoidance). Thus, a minority whose ideological demands cannot be mistaken will have *least* influence on those responses which could be directly associated with it.

At this point, we can make use of Moscovici's explanation of the difference between the extent of influence exerted by majorities and minorities, which is that the former act primarily on those responses most directly associated with themselves, while the latter, in contrast, act on those responses least directly associated with their own explicit position. Confronted with a majority, subjects ask themselves "Why am I different from the rest?" and will tend to minimize the difference. This is a simple process of social comparison leading to the readjustment of responses, but the issue itself is not necessarily questioned. Confronted with a minority, the alternative norm presented forces subjects to attend to the issue, by virtue of its innovatory nature alone. Furthermore, it is possible to argue that rigid style in a minority will make the conflictual nature of its relationship with the population salient, causing the subjects to refuse to cede, while yet engaging them in a certain amount of cognitive work which will later reveal itself in changes in the judgements they have to make which are less directly associated with the minority. That is, of course, unless the conflict is so sharp as to suppress concurrent cognitive activity. A flexible minority, on the other hand, in so far as it induces a lesser conflict, will have greater influence on judgements directly referring to itself (since identification with it is more possible), but this degree of influence in itself may entail lesser cognitive activity at other levels.

Although direct minority/population confrontations are essential for us to be able to determine the nature of the conflict induced and therefore the level at which influence is exerted, we must at the same time emphasize that the effects of flexibility or of rigidity are not direct effects of these variables *per se* but depend crucially upon the perceived meaning of the situation. Thus, if a disagreement is "artificially" induced in a situation, flexibility may well lead to effects more like those of rigidity, in so far as the population's sensitivity to conflict is strongly increased. Similarly, the expectations of the subjects in a particular situation can accentuate the effects of a style: thus negotiations may meet a deadlock sooner if the population had been wrongly expecting a certain amount of reciprocity than if they had known in advance that negotiations were useless. A style may be more or less justified; if it is not justified by the particular situation, then there may be an aggravation of conflict, with all the consequences that this can have for the nature of the influence eventually occurring.

A more direct question we may ask is: what are the consequences of these different styles, in different situations, for the population's cognitive representation of the minority?

5. Minority influence is determined by the population's image of the minority; this image is closely tied to the minority's style of behaviour

Once the consistent minority, and the limits of its position, have been perceived, the population still has to give some meaning and significance to its behaviour. To be able to do this, the population need to elaborate some cognitive representation of the minority. This representation may have several dimensions: physical, aesthetic, intellectual, cognitive, affective, political, social, interactional, etc., each of which may have different weights. A dimension having particular weight will be the minority's perceived attitude toward negotiation: the extent of influence will depend directly on the weighting given to this dimension in the population's image of the minority, formed during the course of interaction with it. Thus it follows that a more rigid style, by accentuating conflict, will give salience to a dimension indicating the degree of negotiation-blocking behaviour. Other dimensions (for instance those relative to perceived consistency) will correspondingly lose weight. Conversely a more flexible style, in so far as it avoids increasing conflict, will avoid making this negative dimension salient.

The effect of a rigid style on the population's image of the minority has an important further consequence. This is not merely a modification of the content of the image, rigidity leading to the perception of negative traits relating to negotiation, and flexibility leading to the perception of favourable traits; rather, it is the structure of the image which is affected. In a negative image, not only have particular negotiation-blocking behaviours become more salient, but they have become a point of reference around which all the other dimensions of the image have been structured. This is a kind of halo effect in which the value connotations of all the dimensions are a function of the connotation (usually negative) acquired by negotiation-blocking behaviour. This is one explanation of the correlations which have been obtained in several experiments among several different dimensions of the image formed of a rigid minority. Thus, consistency may go unrecognized precisely to the extent that rigidity is a salient dimension.

But the image of the minority which has been generated does not act in isolation: it can only have an effect through the categorization of the minority which it induces. A rigid minority, for instance, is often categorized as dogmatic. Such a categorization would of itself justify the rejection, at least the overt rejection, of a minority position. "Dogmatism" in fact entails the existence of a minority which excludes all positions except its own; since the population feels excluded from the outset by virtue of this fact alone, the question of negotiation with the minority simply never arises. It is in such ways that minority positions are perceived—not as consequences of situations in all their variability, but as idiosyncratic and inherent properties of minority identities. We shall return to this point later.

It is important to emphasize here that rigid minority behaviours do not inevitably lead to categorization of the minority as dogmatic, and therefore as alien, not a realistic alternative. In fact, identical minority behaviours can give rise to different images in different situations, and thus the same style of behaviour can have radically different effects.

6. All other things being equal, the population's image of the minority will determine the nature of the minority's influence

Minority behaviour does not take place in a neutral environment: situations are crucial. They are crucial because they facilitate certain images over others, whether the dominant image (cf. our next point), or one determined by the immediate environment of the minority influence attempt. Thus the population may have knowledge of the opinion of certain other persons, which will then serve as a reference point for the creation of an image. It is in this way that the knowledge of judgements already made about the minority's negotiating stance will make the population sensitive to this stance and thus begin the creation of an image in the way described in the previous section. The risks of such a situation, in which the population has definite expectations about minority behaviour, are as we have already indicated: if a relatively flexible style is expected but the behaviour turns out to be rigid, it may be categorized as dogmatic to a greater extent than it would have been otherwise.

The population's image of the minority does not necessarily have to involve definite content for identical minority behaviours to give rise to very dissimilar effects. This is certainly the case in societies in which the mass media invariably condemn minority movements as "disruptive". Conversely, different minority behaviours can give rise to identical effects, depending simply on the categorization induced. We have already seen the importance of the salience of certain dimensions within the image; it is sufficient, then, to induce a more unidimensional perception of the minority, which will render one dimension more salient, for the expected effects to occur. If a population is led to use a large number of categories in its judgements of others, it will be less sensitive to certain behaviours (in particular those which tend to block negotiation) than a population which has been led to use only a few categories, which will in all probability be the most salient ones. The appeal of such a mechanism is easily seen: it permits relatively precise predictions about the receptivity of different populations to different minority styles. Those populations who, in specified situations, use fewest categories will be most sensitive to the appearance of blocking behaviours. Thus, it is not only the ideological preconceptions of a population which are determining, but also their modes of perception of social relations. It may be noted in passing that this is a point of articulation which could facilitate the study of minority effects on the different sub-populations indicated in Figure 1. Without wishing to discuss it in detail here, this point underlines the importance of possession of precise knowledge of the characteristics of the subpopulation studied. Thus, an apparently progressive population may in reality be very sensitive to minority styles of negotiation: students of psychology, for instance, may, as a result of their professional training, make use of rather few categories. This tendency could also be stronger in fully fledged professionals than in students, or in clinical psychologists than in social psychologists, who may be more likely to take situational factors into account. Our theoretical conception may then (general though it is) be able to explain inverted effects: this is one instance of the power of an articulated approach to psychosociological phenomena.

We have now reached one of the nodal points of our theory. The modes of perception we have been discussing (those induced by the situation, by membership in a sub-population, etc.) are crucial in so far as they provide populations with causal theories of minority behaviours. Such theories, however, lie on a continuum rather than existing as discrete entities. At one extreme, consistent minority behaviours are attributed to inherent characteristics of members of the minority. This is exactly the case where a categorization has been made in terms of dogmatism: the population attributes the relevant behaviours to an internal cause (which means, of course, that they are not attributed to the situation). At the other extreme, minority consistency (even rigidity) are attributed to dimensions other than idiosyncratic personal characteristics. A perception which is not monolithic (the term is Ricateau's, 1970–1971) but multidimensional implies a much more differentiated and subtle attribution to a whole set of causes, some of which could arise from the situation. Thus, for instance, minority behaviours could easily be interpreted as being necessitated by a relationship of antagonism. Furthermore, the variety of dimensions increases the probability of recognizing points in common between the minority and the population, hence facilitating identification.

It is vital to add to what has gone before about the effects of minority rigidity that these will only appear when the situation (or other factors) impel the population to interpret minority behaviours in terms of internal properties of the minority members. Several minorities may defend a similar point of view in a rigid manner yet not induce the usual effects of rigidity if they are viewed as being independent of each other. Of course this only applies in the case where minority population relations do not exceed a certain level of conflict, beyond which the relationship is broken off altogether. Similarly, if social antagonisms become too violent, and are marked by strong repression, other mechanisms come into play. In such conditions, our conceptualization predicts that the social cost of any possible identification with the minority becomes too high, and leads to strong avoidance behaviours.

One of the consequences of a multidimensional perception of the minority is that the content of the image itself is not seen as the uniquely determining factor in the minority's behaviour. Although the most usual perception of rigidity attributes it to internal biased causes, it is nevertheless a possibility that even rigidity perceived as such does not bring about the usual effects of rigidity, if this is not attributed solely to inherent characteristics of the minority. Such an outcome is possible if the population is centred, not on inherent properties of the minority, but on the content of the minority's communications (a situation which is bound to create a larger number of dimensions of judgement).

It would appear, then, that the processes of minority influence are extremely complex, even if our theory seems capable of accounting for very varied effects. Given this complexity, how is it possible to explain a certain systematicity which is discernible in the effects of rigidity?

7. Power creates cognitive representations which serve to mask relations of power and of antagonism

Power always has institutional means at its disposal for regulating social deviance. Confronted with the deviance of an active minority, these institutions may respond either repressively, or ideologically, even though most often these two responses are combined. In the case where repression is used, there is a great risk of rendering explicit the relationship of antagonism and its corollary, dominance, in which the population is held. In such a situation, if the population were to identify with the minority in a shared experience of antagonism *vis-à-vis* power, there would be a real danger of power being toppled. There are several examples of this in recent history alone.

For this reason, whenever possible power prefers ideological means of social regulation, usually by providing the population with a system of representation which permits it to perceive a relationship which is, ultimately, one of antagonism, in terms which are very distant from antagonism, and therefore from a power relationship. Thus, the population is "trained" to interpret such relationships through categories of judgement which, having no explicit link with antagonism or power, serve to mask them.

Naturalization is the most general mode of judgement to occur in response to these subtle pressures. The mechanism of naturalization consists in destroying the credibility of a minority by imputing its consistent behaviours to "natural" (or rather "naturalized") characteristics. These are seen as stable, idiosyncratic, unique characteristics belonging to the minority, and more important, as the explanation of their behaviour: their position in a relationship of antagonism is therefore not seen as a possible explanation of their behaviour. Naturalization can take several forms. One is biologism, whereby the causes of behaviour are sought in the biology of the minority (they are blacks, they are women, etc.). Another, and one of the most common, is psychologism (it is their personality, they are paranoid, they are immature, etc.) and the related sociopsychologism (it is the revolt against parents, the generation gap, etc.). It is even possible to imagine sociologism (they are trade unionists, politicians, etc.).

Although this is only one step in the development of our theory, it is interesting to consider the following example of a naturalizing interpretation, which displays in a single instance the variety of ways in which relations of dominance and power relations can be masked (Grounauer, 1977). In 1976, Jean Ziegler, a Swiss sociologist and National Councillor (equivalent of a British Member of Parliament) published a book entitled *Switzerland Above All Suspicion* in which he castigated what has been called "Swiss imperialism". The book quickly became well known and led to a political crisis which was interesting on several counts. There was an initial period in which efforts were made merely to discourage dissemination of the book, but this quickly developed into the use of repressive measures which caused an outcry in a country which had thought itself democratic. However, repression of this kind (the refusal of his university to promote him, for instance) was an implicit confirmation of the charges made in the book. The last phase or the affair, but by no means the least, was the cessation of open repression (his promotion was finally allowed in response to protests by his supporters) in favour of more subtle procedures: there began not only a systematic denigration of the work, which now came to be seen as a tissue of inaccuracies (essentially in the figures used—the classic criterion of scientific validation!—here we are not far from the epistemo-ideology we have already referred to) but also a denigration of the very personality of the sociologist. The following quotation is from a Geneva newspaper, reporting the speech of a Federal Councillor (Minister):

A FAMILY HISTORY

Evidently referring to the book by Genevan National Councillor Ziegler, though without mentioning any names, Mr Chevallaz said "It sometimes happens that a child brought up with love and care in the best of families . . . leaves the table without permission, breaks the best china, slams doors, and goes and tramples on the roses lovingly tended by his grand-mother. Fifty-year-olds start behaving like children, and respectable bankers lose control of their tempers . . . Since Freud, psychologists have explained it many times. Mauriac wrote a novel about it. But the Swiss won't make a drama out of it."

(*La Suisse*, 18 June 1976, page 17.)

Here we see naturalization in operation: the problem, a conflict within a relationship of antagonism, is transformed into a personal pathology explicable by sociological factors (he is a petit bourgeois), his personal relationships (it is a revolt against his family), and his psychodynamic problems (which Freud knew all about). The intention is clear—"The Swiss won't make a drama out of it". Indirectly, this case illustrates well the plausibility of our scheme relating social context and complex relationships: the attempt to mask the real social cause of the denunciation of Swiss imperialism is aimed at preventing the Population (literally, the population of Switzerland) from accepting Ziegler's information at its face value. Clearly, *the danger is not Ziegler so much as his possible influence*! It is worth pointing out that other political regimes have institutionalized the psychopathologization of political deviance.

The processes of minority influence, then, take place within a network of relationships among groups occupying different social positions. Ideological representations are diffused through the population in order to explain and justify these relationships. There is a set of social norms (which are, as we have seen, for good reason partially shared by the whole population) which will certainly determine the course of influence relationships.

8. Perception of the minority is filtered through social norms: there is a bias toward naturalization

Situations of minority influence do not exclude all other social relationships: they take their direction from already existing relationships of power and antagonism. In addition, norms of an ideological nature (such as the naturalization of social deviance as a means of rejecting it) orient and determine perceptions of the minority.

A social norm of naturalization helps explain the regularity with which rigid minority behaviours give rise to certain otherwise inexplicable effects. Confronted with such styles, populations tend to organize their image of the minority around the perception of blockages in negotiation, and to attribute these to internal, natural causes. This type of naturalization has not in fact been unknown during the course of the experiments which have given rise to our theory. By presenting themselves as members of a psychological institute, the experimenters were easily able to set up the desired situations; furthermore, the frequent use of psychological measures and the direction of subjects' attention to characteristics of the minorities tended to facilitate the appearance of a naturalization process. But the main reason why we have found such a concept necessary is that it is possible, as we have seen, to strongly modify the effects of rigidity: thus, for example, when a population judges a minority on political criteria alone, the minority's influence is markedly greater than when the population has been induced to use psychological criteria in addition to political ones. We have also seen that the direction of subjects' attention to psychological characteristics brings about the effects usually associated with rigidity, but this is not the case if attention is directed to the content of communications and the minority identity of their source is not mentioned.

At this point we must be more specific about the nature of perceptions of the minority. We have said, in effect, that an increase in the number of dimensions can have the effect of making blocking behaviours less salient. This is the case, however, only when the dimensions concerned are psychological: when the number of dimensions is increased more generally, the above effect can be reversed. This happens, for instance, when a psychological axis is superimposed on the political one. Predictions about specific situations must give due weight to the possible intervention of one or other form of naturalization.

We should note also that common sense tends to confirm that the use of political labels has the effect of creating more categorical resistance to influence. Such effects can be well accounted for within our explanation: in fact these political labels are referable to naturalizing categories, since minority positions are simply imputed to the existence of the minority group itself, as if its label actually made it into a natural category. Reference to politics does not, then, necessarily reduce the usual effects of rigidity. However, the situation may prevent such attributions being made (this happened, as we shall see later, in several experiments, when a text was not explicitly associated with a minority position).

There is one remaining nodal point of our theory to be explored: why does the rejection of minority influence occur overwhelmingly in relation to judgements which are directly associated with explicit minority positions? Two recent theories in social psychology can account for this, and in so doing create an interesting extension within the theory of social influence itself.

Moscovici has laid stress on the following observation: minority behaviours are given different interpretations in different social contexts: in some, they are welcomed and praised as being original; in others they are condemned as deviant. Thus positive connotations—novelty, progressivism—are as possible as negative ones—marginal, deviant, abnormal, etc. Eiser and Stroebe's theory of social judgements (1972) allows some exact predictions: when a minority position has positive connotations (for example in terms of social originality), the social expression of a movement towards the position is favoured; but when, as is more usual, the minority position has negative connotations (as of deviance, for instance) such an expression is made difficult if not impossible (especially when reprisals are threatened).

The extension of this conceptualization of social judgements to the processes of social influence makes way for a kind of global reinterpretation of the often diverse effects of rigidity, as of flexibility, in different situations. Thus, the effects usually associated with rigidity may well appear whenever minority positions are clearly perceived as such, and therefore as deviant; while, in situations where the character of the minority is concealed or implicit, or the attention of the population is focussed on the content of minority communications, the barriers are down and influence may appear more clearly and be more openly expressed.

Does not flexibility in minority behaviours lead to precisely this result? By making concessions and compromises the flexible minority avoids making explicit its minority character, and therefore avoids activating the minority's anti-deviance norms. However, such flexibility is likely to produce a lesser influence than a rigid style on judgements indirectly associated with the minority position. We shall see in later chapters that this result can be given several different interpretations, but for the moment it is possible to suggest that overt influence is only won at the cost of a certain compromise (frequently ideological, as we have seen). If this is the case, what is likely to happen in the longer term, when the minority is forced at some point to make its position explicit in terms of its conflict with the population? Will the effects of rigidity then appear after all? Will the felt identity come to be seen as having been a mere illusion based upon compromise? This is indeed a major problem for social movements who wish to expand quickly and who therefore accept the costs of compromise, knowing that they have credibility only so long as their more radical positions are not made explicit. On the other hand, does not identification with a rigid minority assure greater cohesion (and therefore diachronic and synchronic consistency) since the identification is based on an ideological acceptance of clear-cut positions? But here also there are multiple constraints on possible outcomes due to situations, and to minority aims and strategies. Our theory predicts certain effects, at least in the short or medium term.

One final question remains: is it possible that explicit, rigid, or naturalized minorities have so little explicit influence (relative, of course, to the influence they have at a different level) because what influence amounts to is a re-definition of a psychosocial identity? In dealing with this question, we shall appeal to a different theory proposed by Tajfel and Turner (in Tajfel, 1978).

9. Influence behaviours define a new psychosocial identity

As Tajfel and his co-workers have shown, the identity of an individual is not composed only of the person's particular and idiosyncratic characteristics. Category membership and group affiliation are also major components of identity.

Thus social identity is a sum of the social memberships of the individual. This individual belongs (or desires to belong) to certain social groups or certain social categories. In relation to each of these, the individual elaborates (and is continuously elaborating) norms of behaviour, representation, and evaluation. Identification with a particular category or group thus signifies the self-attribution of stereotypical characteristics as defined by oneself. We are in agreement with Turner (1981), who considers that influence processes consist in the attribution to the self of stereotypical behaviours, representations, and values of that group which is salient in the psychosocial setting.

Looking at minority influence from this viewpoint, it would appear that the acceptance of minority influence amounts to the attribution to the self of stereotypical minority characteristics, and hence to a redefinition of one's identity *vis-à-vis* both the (former) self and the society.

When affiliation to the minority group has negative connotations, such an identification will be avoided. This would be the case when the minority group is perceived as deviant, for example, when its behaviours are not flexible or when the situation is such that the minority group is perceived through the filter of the dominant ideology. These mechanisms are brought more strongly into play when the situation makes identity itself into a salient issue: minority communications may clearly be concerned with the regulation of group membership, as for instance when the issue is presented as a literal programme of action which a person must agree to by signing and thus becoming a member of the minority. On the other hand, these mechanisms can equally be avoided if subjects are led to perceive that they have certain category memberships in common with the minority.

*   *   *

Thus the circle is complete . . . Taking as our point of departure the styles of minority behaviours and the cognitive processes entailed by these, we were led to consider the interindividual relationships (immediate, or mediated through more distant modes of communication) which are implied by the notion of negotiation styles. These styles give rise to specific images or perceptions, and thus we have arrived at the question of the sociological (for want of a better term) determination of these cognitive (again for want of a less unidimensional term) processes, in our attempt to analyse the subtle operations of the ideological representations which mask social relations of dominance and antagonism. Finally, our hypothesis that influence behaviours may, in certain situations, redefine the psychosocial identity of the individual, has meant a return (paradoxically, it might be said) to the level of the individual via the notion of norms.

All of this is complex and may appear to be nothing more than juggling with abstractions. Yet it is equally apparent that no satisfactory explanation is likely to be produced from analysis confined to a single level—whether individual psychology, social psychology, or sociology. None of these, alone, can account for the subtlety and lability of the processes we have been considering. It is only by beginning to frame explanations which articulate these different levels with each other that we can gain a purchase on the extreme subtlety of these processes. Furthermore, it is precisely here that experimentation becomes a valuable instrument: it allows us to probe directly these points of articulation, by simplifying situations and manipulating one, or few processes at a single time. Thus, experimentation helps us to simplify, but we must also return to theory to bring order and conceptualization into our view of a reality so complex that we are perhaps too ambitious in hoping to model and understand it. The psychosociological theory of minority influence that we have presented may well be interpreted in this way, and our only success may have been to introduce doubts into the mind of the reader. However, the reader can at least judge the empirical basis of our conception, in the experiments which follow.

Part Two

Experimental Illustration

3

Paradigms and methods

1. Psychosociological articulation and experimentation

The essential aim of the psychosociological approach is to grasp the complex articulations among various levels of analysis. This is why experimentation offers a specially useful means to illustrate our "articulation" theory of the diffusion of minority innovations. Other means, which would certainly have been much more clostly, could have been used: field observations, a monograph-type study, and so on. However, for our particular theory, the study of specific cases is not the most comprehensive method of attack. A single case, at best, can only exemplify one of the multiple articulations which are theoretically possible; while a series of experiments permits the careful manipulation of all these possibilities. Nevertheless, consideration of situations as they occur "in the field", without any intervention, is a valuable adjunct; this gives a measure of the plausibility and interpretative significance of a theory.

An articulation theory of the type we are proposing does have certain methodological implications. First of all, it suggests mistrust of the type of simple effects (statistical ones, that is) which can be easily replicated. Thus, if the initial experiments show that a rigid minority exerts less influence than a flexible one, it must be concluded either that this is a truism without much scientific interest, or that it is a truism masking processes which we have not yet understood. *Ultimately , it is only by negating—perhaps even reversing but at least by modifying an effect—that we are able to appreciate its full extent and significance.*

By using the word articulation we mean it to be understood that the effect of one variable (flexibility versus rigidity, for example) differs according to the value or sign of another variable (for example, whether the social norm activated in the situation favours an originality or a deviance interpretation of minority behaviour). What we are seeking therefore is an interaction, in the statistical sense, rather than simple effects. Such an interaction can take place within a single level, as for instance in the case when the effect of rigid or flexible negotiation is modulated by whether agreement or disagreement exists between population and minority. However, this would not be an articulation in the theoretical sense we intend: an interaction is not properly articulative unless there is an interaction between two variables from two different levels of analysis, as in the first case given above, in which the effect of negotiation may vary according to the normative context.

Such interactions are not confined within the setting of a single experiment (from the point of view of statistical analysis). They can appear between experiments, *to the extent that the sequence of experiments is designed hypothetico-deductively to shed light on the articulation theory.* In fact, it would be impossible to arrange the articulations theoretically possible within a single experiment. The theory must be judged, then, on the basis of a sequence of related experiments. This is so true that a single experiment by itself demonstrates nothing, and local reinterpretations in terms of alternative theories are only rejected, often because they fail to make sense of the larger experimental picture. Thus, occasionally an individual experiment has given us the feeling that we could have, or ought to have, controlled or manipulated certain other variables or added some other condition. In these cases it is important to bear in mind that each experiment must be seen within a wider context.

The foregoing points should indicate that we have carefully evaluated the costs and benefits of our methodology. We are aware of many experiments which have taken a year or two years to conduct. It is important to evaluate the costs and benefits of these: does the theoretical interest justify such a large investment? A choice has to be made. Ours was to seek validity in the theoretical interlocking of a series of experiments rather than in the intrinsic features of the individual experiment, which are too often the exclusive focus of those "art critics" of science, the methodologists.

2. The experimental sequence

A set of fifteen experiments is grouped into four chapters. A first phase reports three experiments which study the effects in very different con-

texts of various minority styles (flexible or rigid) on the degree of influence and on the population's perception of the minority. Once these
effects are established, we seek in the second phase to modulate them
by manipulating certain intrasituational aspects, which are essentially
to do with the social relationships within which flexibility and rigidity
are studied. The third phase focuses on the mechanisms determining
the perception of the minority; the importance of this aspect of the
influence process will have been established in the first two phases.
Experiments in the third phase create situations in which we induce
different perceptions of a minority, according to whether it behaves
flexibly or rigidly. The fourth phase directly articulates the mechanisms
previously demonstrated with social norms, activated in a variety of
situations. Finally, we attempt to articuate social norms with intra-
situatonal negotiations. At this point, we hope to illustrate the link
between social influence and psychosocial identity which is integral to
the relationships between groups.

The intervention of social norms was very obvious in our first experiments which dealt with intrasituational variables. However, it was
only later, after we had gained some control over the effects usual in
the types of situation we set up, that we were able to manipulate the
effects of these social norms directly.

3. Paradigms and procedures

More than half the experiments reported used the same materials and
procedure, differing only in the specific variables relevant to each
experiment. This paradigm will be described here in detail, so as to
avoid repetition later when each experiment is reported individually.
(It should be noted, however, that other paradigms were also used.
Three experiments (1, 2 and 9) had the Swiss national army as their
subject. The procedure in each of these experiments was fundamen-
tally different and will be reported at the same time as the experiments
themselves. Two of these experiments are the first to be reported, and
the third is particularly simple in terms of its materials and procedure,
so this manner of reporting should clarify matters in appropriate
steps. A fourth experiment, concerned with attitudes towards "guest-
workers", is described in detail on pp. 138–146.

All the remaining experiments used the "pollution" paradigm,
which we describe in detail now.

(A) QUESTIONNAIRE

The opinion questionnaire concerned the attribution of responsibility for pollution. There were about twenty propositions, randomly ordered, and remaining constant throughout. Although the individual propositions were randomly ordered, the items fell into five categories, as follows:

> four accused industry of being responsible for pollution (IR)
> four blamed social categories (CR)
> four denied that industry was to blame (NI)
> four denied that social categories were to blame (NC)
> four blamed both industry and social categories for pollution, but they were not actually used in the assessment of opinions and had been included only to relieve the monotony of the other items' unilateral emphasis.

Each item category referring to industry mentioned the following industries once each: detergents, automobiles, chemicals, and chemical fertilizers. Symmetrically, each of the following social categories was mentioned once among the other items (CR and NC): householders, drivers, picnickers, and farmers. Table 1 gives the complete questionnaire.

TABLE 1

Questionnaire on responsibility for pollution (the scale is illustrated for the first item only here)

---

1. Householders are very much to blame: they use washing powders and the most polluting detergents in a completely inconsiderate manner:

    AGREE   1   2   3   4   5   6   7   DISAGREE

2. Car manufacturers take active and effective steps against pollution: they invest enormous sums in producing the cleanest possible cars.

3. It is completely unrealistic to blame washing-powder manufacturers, because their products are not harmful if they are used according to the instructions given.

4. Both the users and the producers of washing powders are to blame, in equal measure, for water pollution.[a]

5. The problem of pollution will never be solved as long as motorists cannot even be induced to switch off their engines during prolonged stops, at red traffic lights, etc.

6. Supermarkets and the manufacturers of chemical fertilizers have no scruples about denaturing natural products.[b]

7. Campers who light fires in woodland without proper precautions and firms who build factories in the open countryside are equally to blame: both risk destroying the balance of nature.[a]

8. How can we blame farmers when we know perfectly well that if they don't use chemical fertilizers, even against their will, they will be forced out of business?[b]

9. People who blame picnickers and day-trippers for the degradation of nature are only trying to deflect attention from the real problems and the real guilt.[b]

10. Factories built in the countryside are always at a carefully spaced distance from each other, so as to avoid concentrations; this shows a real respect for nature.

11. The automobile industries are only concerned with profit: not only do they refuse to take part in the struggle against pollution, but by insisting on increasing their output they are among those most responsible for it.[b]

12. It must be acknowledged that chemical fertilizer manufacturers have spent large sums in research to find products which increase yield while conserving the natural qualities of agricultural produce.

13. Whether making vehicles or driving them, the responsibility is the same: enormous.[a]

14. Day-trippers, with their careless attitude and behaviour, have a grave responsibility for the slow but irreversible deterioration of nature.

15. Farmers, in their short-sighted and selfish use of more and more chemical fertilizers, are giving us poorer and poorer quality produce.

16. Washing-powder manufacturers must accept the responsibility for continuing to sell (and advertise) products whose harmful properties they are fully aware of.[b]

17. It is simply lying to accuse drivers of being the most to blame for pollution.[b]

18. We should resist the attempts made to blame householders, when they are in fact only the victims of glossy advertizing which conceals the harmfulness of the products sold.[b]

19. Farmers and the producers of chemical fertilizers are in an open alliance for profit, while the quality of the produce deteriorates.[a]

20. Heavy industries recognize only criteria of profit and convenience in siting their factories, while nature is damaged by the fumes and dust they disgorge.[b]

---

[a] These items blame both industries and social categories and are not included in the assessment of opinions

[b] These are the items most directly associated with the minority position presented in the text (*direct* items)

Unmarked items are the least directly associated with the minority position, since they do not appear in the text (*indirect* items)

The questionnaire focused on the issue of whether blame for pollution should lie with industry or with certain social categories. However, also implicit in the issue is the further one of whether the politico-economic system is responsible or whether responsibility lies with individuals (here inferred from the categories of people—householders, drivers, etc.).

One result stemming from the questionnaire which we should mention at the outset is that populations tended to accept initially (i.e. at the time of pre-test) the set of opinions as given. That is, they certainly agreed that industry was to blame, but they also accepted that social categories were responsible. The goal of minority influence, then, was to convince populations that industry alone was to blame and that the accusations against social categories were merely pretexts to mask the real locus of responsibility: the politico-economic system.

As Table 1 indicates, in response to each proposition the subjects were to encircle one figure out of a scale from 1 (agree totally) to 7 (totally disagree) to correspond to their own opinion. By taking the mean of the four items relevant to each of the four categories (IR, CR, NI and NC) it was possible to assess the extent of agreement.

What interested us most, of course, was the extent of change. This also was very easily assessed. After their initial response to the questionnaire, subjects read a text which placed blame exclusively on industry and denied that social categories had any responsibility whatsoever. They then responded again to the same questionnaire. The extent of influence was assessed by comparing the pre-test and post-test scores for each item category, as follows:

If subjects *accept more* IR items (by having a mean score closer to 1 on the post-test than on the pre-test), there has been positive influence;

The same holds for the NC items;

If subjects *reject more* CR items (by having a post-test mean score closer to 7 than on pre-test), there has been positive influence;

The same holds for the NI items.

We were thus able to obtain a global measure of influence. However, as has already been indicated, it was expected that minority influence would be expressed differently according to the type of item. Thus, the IR and NC items should be affected similarly in so far as they are both directly associated with the minority position defended in the text—we term these *direct* items. Similarly, the CR and NI items formed a unity, in that they represented a position which was not defended (rather, implicitly rejected) in the minority discourse. Since these items were not directly associated with the minority position, we term them *indirect*.

All the tables give mean changes on a 7-point scale (with the exception of experiments 10 and 14, which used an 11-point scale), the sign indicating the direction of change. Means are given separately for *direct* and *indirect* items.

(B) PROCEDURE

In most of the experiments, the procedure followed the sequence pre-test, experimental phase, then post-test. Before the pre-test, the experimenters introduced themselves as university research workers testing a new technique of opinion polling. The subjects were then given the questionnaire, which they responded to individually. The confidentiality of these responses was assured, although subjects' names and school class membership were needed to compare individual responses over the different phases of the experiments. Most of the experiments were conducted in classrooms.

The experimental phase was the focus of interest, since it was at this point that the independent variables producing influence effects were to be manipulated. This phase will be described in detail as each experiment is reported individually. There was, however, one constant feature in (almost) all the experiments: during this phase, the subjects received a text (the source of influence) which accused industry of the sole responsibility for pollution, while rejecting any blame on the part of social categories. This phase generally took place one week after the pre-test, and immediately before the post-test.

The third phase was essentially concerned with a second response to the opinion questionnaire. The ostensible reason given to subjects for this was that the reading of a related text often allows people to clarify their opinions. Subjects then filled in a further questionnaire about the image they had formed of the source; this questionnaire will be reproduced later. The session ended with an interview. We will refer to this only rarely, since the questions posed were only marginally related to our theoretical interests.

Finally, we held a de-briefing session, during which we explained the reasons for the research and the form it had taken.

(C) THE INFLUENCE SOURCE (TEXT)

During the experimental phase, subjects read a text which placed blame squarely on industry and with equal firmness denied any responsibility on the part of social categories. The nature of this text can be seen in Table 2, where it is reproduced in full. Why did we use such a text? Because it can in fact be claimed that power, while officially acknowledging that industry is responsible, nevertheless more often obscures this by focusing attention on individual responsibility through the device of raising the question of the role of social categories, ostensibly as a kind of contrast case. This device makes sense particularly in the context of school activities. When we carried out our first experiments, vast campaigns of litter collection and the cleaning-up of particular sites were being organized. We are not concerned here with a detailed discussion of the social representations involved in the issue of pollution, but it should be emphasized that the position which attaches blame solely to the politico-economic system and absolves individuals of any responsibility, is a minority one. It is a minority position not only in relation to power, but also in relation to some ecological movements which *also* attach importance to individual action.

TABLE 2
Influence text used in the pollution paradigm

(A)
Hardly a week goes by without pollution being mentioned on TV or in the newspapers. The problem is already serious, but pollution is getting worse day by day. It is vital to act now, not only to clean up existing pollution but also to prevent the spread. But if we are going to do this, we must know the causes of it. Who is responsible? INDUSTRY IS THE MAIN CULPRIT BECAUSE OF ITS UNBRIDLED AND UNHEEDING PURSUIT OF PROFIT

(B)
We know what harm is done by exhaust fumes (a car leaves about 5000 m^3 of polluting fumes and 10 kg of dust for every 1000 km it travels). The automobile industry is willing to poison the air of towns and even the countryside, using outrageous advertising techniques to push products designed only to rake in profits. Motorists are helpless in this situation. Cars could easily be equipped with anti-pollution filters which would fit simply on the exhaust system, yet manufacturers refuse to do this because it would cost them money.
WE SHOULD BAN MANUFACTURERS WHO DO NOT RESPECT REGULATIONS[1]

(C)
Attempts have been made to blame picnickers and day-trippers for pollution, by launching clean-up and litter campaigns. But these are only ways of hiding the true culprits. How can we compare the few bits of litter and empty containers left behind by day-trippers with the tons of fumes, toxic gas and dust belched out over huge areas by factories?
WE SHOULD BAN ALL POLLUTING INDUSTRIES[2]

(D)

Householders are frequently and wrongly accused of polluting water. We should not overlook the fact that the washing powders they use are made by a chemical industry which takes little interest in the harm that they do as long as they wash whiter and faster and are used as much as possible. The race for profits pushes industry into making more and more products that they are obliged to sell by any means possible, such as dishonest advertising, and "bargain offers" that deceive consumers.
THE INDUSTRIAL PRODUCTION OF WASHING POWDERS SHOULD BE STOPPED AT ONCE[3]

(E)

Farmers are just as often blamed for using too much chemical fertilizer in order to increase their yields. But they are obliged to do this if they want to keep their livelihood. The real responsibility lies with the supermarket chains and the fertilizer producers, who have no scruples about denaturing food products (in other words about sacrificing quality to financial gain).
FACTORIES WHICH CAUSE POLLUTION SHOULD BE MADE TO CEASE PRODUCTION AT ONCE[4]

The slogans given in this table are rather *rigid*; in order to have a more *flexible* text, we replaced slogans 1 to 4 with the following:

1. CAR MANUFACTURERS SHOULD BE OBLIGED TO DELIVER CARS ALREADY EQUIPPED WITH ANTI-POLLUTION FILTERS
2. INDUSTRIES WHICH CAUSE POLLUTION SHOULD BE FINED
3. INDUSTRIAL PRODUCTION OF WASHING POWDERS SHOULD BE REGULATED
4. FACTORIES WHICH GIVE OUT POLLUTION WASTE SHOULD BE FINED

The paragraphs are labelled A to E to make methodological details clearer.

The text is organized in five paragraphs. In most of the experiments, the first paragraph (A in Table 2) emphasizes the spread and urgency of the pollution problem. Who is to blame? The remaining four paragraphs answer this question by outlining a series of minority views:

(B) Drivers are the victims of the automotive industries.

(C) What is the significance of the small amount of litter left behind by picnickers, when measured against the pollution created by the chemical industries?

(D) Householders are not responsible, but detergent manufacturers are, because they use all possible means to sell products that they know are harmful.

(E) It is not farmers who are to blame for the denaturing of agricultural produce, but the chemical fertilizer industry and the supermarket chains.

Comparison between the opinion questionnaire and the influence text will show that the four IR items and the four NC items in the questionnaire appear, almost verbatim, in the text. These, of course, are *direct* items, directly associated with the text's case. The other, *indirect*, questionnaire items do not appear in the text. Therefore any influence on them will be the result of inference from explicit items in the text.

(D) MANIPULATION OF FLEXIBILITY AND RIGIDITY

This paradigm does not involve any direct interaction between individuals. Therefore negotiation could only be symbolic and anticipatory—anticipatory because it would be based on pre-existing knowledge of the attitude of the population toward positions which could be characterized as more or less rigid or flexible.

The manipulation of this variable was therefore done by using slogans following each of the four paragraphs B, C, D and E. These slogans were given typographical emphasis, and offered solutions to the problem of pollution. The flexible slogans proposed sanctions and fines for the polluting industries, while the rigid slogans drew extreme consequences from the position they were based on—for instance the immediate stoppage of production, which was an extreme proposal unlikely to be easily assented to by the subjects.

All the slogans are given in Table 2, the rigid slogans in the text and the flexible slogans in the footnote.

(E) MINORITY-IMAGE QUESTIONNAIRE

We have already discussed at length the theoretical importance of the perception of the minority. We designed an instrument to assess subjects' perception of the minority along two dimensions which are central to the theory of minority influence we have put forward. The first dimension is that of consistency, and the second is that of the degree of perceived flexibility or rigidity.

The instrument was a questionnaire which obtained subjects' initial intuitive judgements about the minority source. They chose from a list of 40 adjectives, reproduced in Table 3. Ten of the 40 expressed a positive evaluation in terms of consistency (K); ten expressed a corresponding negative evaluation (I); ten expressed a positive evaluation in terms of flexibility (F); ten expressed a negative evaluation in terms of rigidity (R). Subjects were instructed to place a cross next to the

TABLE 3

Questionnaire assessing perception of the minority source. The letters placed after each adjective indicate the dimension and evaluation it refers to: **K** consistency, **I** inconsistency, **F** flexibility, **R** rigidity

1. arrogant (R)	21. methodical (K)
2. adaptable (F)	22. open (F)
3. authoritarian (R)	23. agreeable (F)
4. changeable (I)	24. balanced (F)
5. assured (K)	25. inconstant (I)
6. confused (I)	26. rational (K)
7. considered (K)	27. realistic (F)
8. cooperative (F)	28. rigid (R)
9. resolute (K)	29. self-confident (K)
10. disordered (I)	30. serious (K)
11. dominant (R)	31. superficial (I)
12. effective (K)	32. unsure (I)
13. rigorous (K)	33. sociable (F)
14. hateful (I)	34. obstinate (R)
15. stubborn (R)	35. likeable (F)
16. hostile (R)	36. tolerant (F)
17. immature (I)	37. hard (R)
18. intolerant (R)	38. understanding (F)
19. irresponsible (I)	39. unfriendly (R)
20. logical (K)	40. unintelligent (I)

adjectives which corresponded to the image they had formed about the source, as a result of reading the text.

We combined the indices as follows in treating the results. For the consistency dimension, we subtracted the number of "inconsistent" (I) adjectives marked from the number of "consistent" (K) adjectives. Similarly, the degree of perceived flexibility or rigidity was assessed by subtracting the number of "rigid" adjectives marked from the number of flexible ones.

We checked the validity of this instrument by asking five judges to classify the 300 adjectives in Gough's (1960) *Adjective Check List* into these four categories, of which definitions were provided, as follows: *consistency*—internal coherence in the response system and firmness of purpose; *inconsistency*—absence of consistency characteristics; *flexibility*—supple social attitude, taking opposing viewpoints into account; *rigidity*—absence of negotiation with others. We retained only those adjectives on which there was unanimous agreement among the judges about its category assignment.

4. Important notes

Before we report the experiments in detail, the following points should be noted:

(1) We do not report in detail the nature of the population sample in each experiment. For the most part these were adolescents of about fifteen years old (in their final year of compulsory schooling or their first year of further or higher education). The sessions were carried out in their normal classrooms, usually in the presence of their teacher, who was a passive observer. We shall not specify such details further unless they are relevant to the particular experiment.

(2) Several of the experiments have already been published as articles or are in press; in these cases, we give the reference at the beginning of the report. In some cases, only part of the original experimental design is included, in accordance with our present theoretical purposes; statistical analysis is done only on the relevant sub-set of data.

(3) Although we report the means of opinion change indicating influence, we do not give details of the statistical analysis we carried out, which for the most part were analyses of variance. To do so would add unnecessarily to the length of the text, without particularly clarifying what we wish to convey. Our sources were Winer (1962) for analyses of variance and Siegel (1956) for non-parametric tests.

(4) We adopted the ·05 level of significance. As far as possible we have held to this, although we have occasionally accepted effects at the ·10 level, when it was possible to suggest a hypothesis for the weakness of an effect.

4

Flexible and rigid negotiation: their effects

Suppose that a minority puts forward a clearly defined position on a social question, such as the army or pollution. Suppose also that the minority's behaviour is consistent, that is to say, over time the same propositions are defended, regardless of the pressures exerted for change, or at least to tone down the position. Such a minority will probably be perceived as consistent. But, as we have seen, consistency alone does not guarantee the power to influence. One of our initial hypotheses was that if the blockage of negotiation which characterizes consistency is perceived by the population as a blockage in the social relationship with itself, then influence will be weak, or even non-existent. This first hypothesis was tested in three experiments which also illustrate the variety of possible operationalizations of flexible and rigid negotiation styles.

In an early experiment we attempted to set up a negotiation (holding consistency constant, of course) which was explicitly confined to formal matters. Without modifying its position, the minority ceded on questions related to the functioning of the group (the establishment of a consensus). In a second experiment, a minority held a position equally consistently but also negotiated, in a flexible or rigid style, on a question of ideological importance. It should also be noted that these first two experiments involved more direct interactions, the minority being physically present in the situation. In the third experiment, in contrast, we used tracts alone to represent the minority. This proved to be less expensive, while losing nothing in terms of theoretical significance. The different negotiation styles were induced by means of slogans which were either very strongly or less strongly against certain opinions which are deeply rooted in our population.

These manipulations produced the type of minority influence which is the focus of our investigation. Fortunately, we had already by the time of the second experiment introduced a measure of the image of the minority, a measure which we use in almost all the later experiments. The use of this measure has proved to be very valuable in understanding the process of minority/population negotiation.

Experiment 1: Formal interpersonal negotiation

Two types of minority can be distinguished, according to their orientation toward social norms. Some can be said to be progressive, in the sense that they support positions which would imply a historical evolution of social norms, in other words, of the existing order. Others could be called reactionary, in so far as they would be opposed to such social change. The mechanisms by which one or other type of minority influences a population appear to vary in several respects (on this subject, see Paicheler, 1976, 1977; Mugny, 1979). It is the first type of minority, the progressives, that interest us in this book. However, a reactionary minority may also illustrate specific points of our theory, and we have used such a minority in our first and our penultimate experiments.

The first experiment still bears the strong imprint of an inter-individual approach to social psychology. Thus, we set up real interactions between three individuals (of whom one was a confederate of the experimenter), and the negotiation was concerned with a collective decision (search for a consensus). At this time, a reactionary minority was chosen, since this represented a position directly opposed to that of our subjects. The minority character was therefore still defined in terms of the rarity (quasi-numerically) of the position concerned. It was not until the second experiment that we developed the idea of the sociological context of innovation, which led to our theory. However, let us look at this first experiment now in detail.

THE EXPERIMENT (MUGNY *ET AL.*, 1972–1973)

The subjects, all volunteers, were users of a leisure centre, and we knew that they held an opinion of the idea of a national army which was relatively unfavourable. These subjects were placed, in pairs, in a situation with a confederate who argued a strongly pro-militarist, and hence minority position.

When the subjects arrived for the session, introductions were made between them, the three experimenters and the confederate in such a way as to convey that the confederate was previously unknown to the experimenters. Two of the experimenters then left to go into another room, from which they could observe the procedure via recording equipment.

(a) The pre-test

Subjects were asked to indicate their opinion about a national army on an 8-point scale from "I am absolutely in favour" to "I am absolutely against". They next responded to six questions which would be the themes of the later discussion, again on an 8-point scale. However, the principal measure was a 40-adjective questionnaire on which subjects were asked to mark those adjectives which corresponded to their own idea of the national army.

These adjectives had been obtained as follows: a large set was presented to about forty judges who were asked to classify them as positive or negative when applied to "national army". From this set we retained 20 positive and 20 negative adjectives. It was then possible to derive an evaluation score for subjects by subtracting the number of negative adjectives they had marked from the number of positive ones. Thus, an extreme anti-militarist position would be indicated by a score of -20, and an extreme pro-militarist position by a score of $+20$. We found that the mean score was around -10 in both experimental conditions, and thus the initial attitude was relatively negative, as we had supposed.

The same questions were put to subjects in the post-test, which allowed us to assess the extent of attitude change.

(b) The experimental phase

The experimental phase followed immediately after the pre-test, and consisted of a discussion among the three subjects (of whom one was the confederate). The experimenter instructed the three to talk for about three minutes on each of the six questions specially put for this purpose in the pre-test. (These questions and the responses to them can be seen in Table 4.) The subjects were simply asked to have a fairly free discussion, and to see whether they could come to some kind of agreement. Before each of these six discussions, they re-read the question and gave a written, as well as a spoken response to it. The experimenter then produced a magnetic board with a letter corresponding to each subject, and the subject's response on the 8-point scale, so that the divergence of opinion was clearly visible to all.

TABLE 4

The six discussion questions and the response scale

Question 1
The majority of the Swiss people wish peace to be maintained. Furthermore, many international organizations working for peace have their headquarters in Switzerland.
  Do you think, taking into account the total context of military and political activity throughout the world, that the money given to the army and to the international organizations should be allocated:
□ totally to the army (100% as against 0%)?
□ overwhelmingly in favour of the army (85% as against 15%)?
□ largely in favour of the army (70% as against 30%)?
□ slightly in favour of the army (60% as against 40%)?
□ slightly in favour of the international organizations (60% as against 40%)?
□ largely in favour of the international organizations (70% as against 30%)?
□ overwhelmingly in favour of the international organizations (85% as against 15%)?
□ totally in favour of the international organization (100% as against 0%)?

Question 4
The ethos being imparted through teaching to the younger generation is now widely questioned. Given the present international context, do you think that teaching should be reoriented so as to make acceptable the following allocation of finance to the army and to the international organizations:
(same sale as for Question 1).

Question 2
Given the present balance of military and political forces (world-wide), do you think that the Swiss national defence budget should be redistributed?
  Is your opinion that it should be:
□ totally redistributed (be 100% less than now)?
□ much diminished (by 75%)?
□ reduced by half (by 50%)?
□ slightly reduced (by 25%)?
□ increased by half (by 50%)?
□ very much increased (by 75%)?
□ doubled (100% more than now)?

Question 5
If we are to continue to pursue the politics of neutrality, does the Swiss army need to be modernized? If so, how should national expenditure on the army be redistributed?
  Is your opinion that it should be:
(same scale as for Question 2)

Question 3
New conceptions in modern armies have led to changes in the length of soldiers' training.
Do you think that the length of service should be:
☐ doubled (100% longer than now)?
☐ significantly increased (75% longer)?
☐ increased by half (50% longer)?
☐ slightly increased (25% longer)?
☐ slightly decreased (25% shorter)?
☐ decreased by half (50% shorter)?
☐ significantly decreased (75% shorter)?
☐ abolished altogether (100% less than now)?

Question 6
The Constitution says that "every Swiss is born a soldier". The responsibilities of the citizen (national defence, maintenance of neutrality, public interest, etc.) may depend on his participation in the army. In this case, how do you think the length of military service should be changed?
Do you think that the length of service should be:
(same scale as for Question 3)

The device also served to emphasize the consistency of the confederate's behaviour. The confederate defended a pro-militarist position using prepared arguments which were based on those used in military tribunals hearing cases of conscientious objectors. In particular, we had prepared answers to certain embarrassing questions which could be foreseen, so as to avoid allowing the discussion to lead into areas where the confederate might lose consistency.

Thus, the confederate's consistency was held constant throughout (a policy which succeeded, as indicated by responses to a post-experimental questionnaire item). The negotiations themselves were manipulated through the confederate's apparent choice of response on the 8-point scale.

(c) Rigidity and flexibility in negotiation

In the two experimental conditions, the confederate gave an extreme pro-militarist response on each of the first three questions. He was therefore totally at odds with the subjects, who responded at the other end of the scale, that is less favourably toward the army.

To fully grasp the nature of the experimental manipulation, it should be recalled that each of the last three questions (4, 5, 6) had the same response scale as each of the first three (1, 2, 3). In the rigid (negotiation-blocking) condition, the confederate continued to give the same extreme response for the last three items. In contrast, in the flexible condition, from the fourth item onwards the confederate stated that since they were all to try to reach agreement, he had better choose a less extreme response. Although insisting that he continued to hold his original beliefs (to emphasize his consistency) he chose a response which was less extreme by two points (from 8 to 6, or from 1 to 3). Thus, the confederate negotiated the conflict, or at least stated that this was his intention, and in a purely formal manner, since he stated that it was in order to facilitate a consensus (which was clearly in reality impossible, owing to the divergence of the original positions) that he was moderating his choices.

At the end of the six three-minute discussions, subjects once more filled in the pre-test questionnaires. Each of them was then interviewed by one of the experimenters, initially with standardized questions but later more informally. Finally, everyone re-assembled in the experimental room, where the confederate's true role was revealed, and the real intention of the experiment. This de-briefing was often followed by discussions, some of them very lengthy.

(d) Results

During the experimental discussions, the subjects' responses were often very close to each other on the same side of the response scale, while the confederate's responses were both more extreme and at the other side of the scale. In one condition, the minority responses were identical throughout the six discussions, in the other they were modified in the last three discussions. What happened during these interactions? In fact the changes were very slight. There was no movement towards the confederate. However, each subject had some social support from the other subject. (On the problem of social support in minority influence, see Doms and Van Avermaet, 1980b.) This coalition often expressed itself through aggression and sarcastic remarks directed at the confederate. Given that this was the case, why was there no polarization of the subjects' responses? One answer to this is that the situation was very constrictive due to the presence of the display which reminded the subjects of their initial responses. Further, to have polarized their responses would have been to widen further the gulf which already separated the discussants, and to increase the discomfort of inter-individual tensions.

If we look for differences in response to the six questions between the pre- and the post-test, again we find no difference. This can also be explained by the presence of the display which reminded subjects of their initial responses, and an experimental procedure which tended to minimize the possibilities for change.

What can be said about the responses less directly related to the discussion? Did release from the constraints of the experimental situation permit any expression of change, and did this differ according to the experimental condition? Responses to the 40-adjective questionnaire were in fact significantly different between the two conditions. The possible scores ranged from $+20$ (strongly in favour of the army) to -20 (strongly opposed to the army), and on pre-test most subjects scored around -10. Table 5 shows the extent of change in evaluation of the army in the two conditions.

Thus, as we had predicted, a flexible minority has more influence than a rigid minority, since the first "ameliorates" responses to the army, while the second further polarizes the initial negative evaluation ($U_{18,18} = 105.5$, one-tailed $P < .05$). If we take the means of the two subjects in each individual group, the result is the same: $U_{9,9} = 19.5$, $P < .05$). However, in a social setting it is not only the mean change which is important: the distribution of changes must also be taken into account. Table 6 therefore gives the numbers of subjects who did not change, who moved toward the minority, and who moved away from the minority.

TABLE 5

Mean influence on evaluation of the army
($n = 18$)

Flexible minority	$+0.83$
Rigid minority	-1.67

TABLE 6

Frequency of subjects who did not change (0), who moved toward the source ($+$), and who moved away from the source ($-$) ($n = 18$)

	$+$	0	$-$
Flexible minority	7	5	6
Rigid minority	2	5	11

It is clear that rigidity brings about a strong polarization: by inducing subjects to reject its positions, the minority exacerbates conflict and brings about a strong categorization effect. It would be tempting to suppose on this basis that flexibility is simply more effective, except that it is seen to lead to a relative lack of differentiation among positions, since some subjects change toward the minority while others move away. This is seen in the fact that the 7 subjects who were influenced positively are distributed across 6 different groups (thus there was only a single group in which both subjects moved toward the minority). We shall see later how flexible negotiation defuses the population's reactions of opposition towards it, by making its position more fluid, and less explicitly adversarial.

Experiment 2: Ideological and anticipatory negotiation

Experiment 2 differs in several respects from Experiment 1.

It is embedded in a rationale which is concerned with the complexity of the social context of innovation; thus it is based on the distinction among the three factors: power, population and minority.

The minority is a progressive one, defined as being in opposition to the dominant norms, and not, as in the first experiment, simply holding a position contradictory to that held by the population.

It takes account of the possibility, not controlled in the first experiment, that two types of process could have interfered with the situation we had intended to create: firstly, the immediate effects of the minority's style, and secondly the social support which the experimental subjects could have afforded each other.

The experimental situation also physically confronts the population with the minority (through one of its representatives), but this time the confrontation takes the form of a speech made by the minority to an audience, whose members do not interact either with the minority or with each other. In other words, there is no possibility here of the interactive, reciprocal negotiation which took place in Experiment 1. *The negotiation is symbolic and anticipatory, based on existing knowledge of the population's ideological preconceptions.* This involves, in effect, anticipating the points of disagreement which will certainly arise between minority and population, and ideological negotiation on these points, either flexibly in discriminating levels of disagreement, or rigidly in maintaining or even aggravating disagreements: in the latter case what takes place is the *ideological* blockage of negotiation.

THE EXPERIMENT (MUGNY, 1975a)

The subjects were forty apprentices aged between 16 and 20. They were members of a leisure centre and volunteered to take part in the experiment. As in the preceding experiment, this population was relatively opposed to the idea of a national army.

(a) Questionnaire

Here we report only the most complete measure used. As in Experiment 1, other questions used did not give results. The questionnaire of interest, then, was composed of 24 propositions and a 7-point rating scale ranging from "left" (1) to "right" (7). For each proposition, the subject was to indicate whether it represented a position politically more to the left or to the right.

The 24 items displayed in Table 7 fall into 4 categories: 7 defend a clearly right-wing position, i.e. pro-militarist; 7 represent a more moderate, but still pro-militarist position ("yes to national defence, but no to an army of repression" is a good example); 10 items defend a clearly left-wing, anti-militarist position.

Because the minority speech defended a frankly anti-militarist stance, close to that of the latter 10 items, we expected that positive influence would be expressed in: a rejection of the right-wing, pro-militarist items; equally strong rejection of the more moderate items, since these do, after all, admit the permanent existence of an army; a shift toward the left, in acceptance of the anti-militarist items. These predictions, in fact, derive directly from Sherif and Hovland's (1965) assimilation/contrast theory, according to which extremism in opinion will be expressed in the extremization of judgements relative to the object of opinion.

The same questionnaire was given both before and after the experimental phase. The difference in response could be measured either globally, or separately for each category of items.

TABLE 7
Questionnaire: Experiment 2 (scale reproduced for first item only)[a]

---

1. YES to national defence, NO to an army of repression—that is our position.

    LEFT 1 2 3 4 5 6 7 RIGHT

2. In the struggle against subversion, we must make an effort to re-evaluate the structure of our society and of our state (the family, the churches, democracy) to satisfy everyone, especially young people.

3. The army forces soldiers into action against all spontaneous demonstrations by the population. This is not so much preparing to defend the "Fatherland", as crushing the legitimate demands of workers.

4. Order, peace, and work—our liberties are priceless. A modern army, even though it is costly, is worth the expense because it is the guarantee of our values.

5. The army buys an enormous amount of goods and materials, and then wastes them in useless exercises. In its economic aspect alone, the army supports the profits of the class in power.

6. The army is an institution which reproduces and even accentuates social and economic inequality.

7. The idea of a "Fatherland" over and above the social classes is a way of making people believe that the interests of workers and of bosses are really the same. Of course it is a lie.

8. We must struggle to make our army more democratic: soldiers must be able to discuss orders and actions if they believe them to be wrong or against their conscience.

9. Expenditure on the army is really too high: there are other socially useful sectors which should receive some of that money, such as new hospitals, schools, etc.

10. The army should assist in the maintenance and reinstatement of law and order; it should be ready to assist the police in this task if necessary.

11. The anti-militarism of the proletariat is only relative, not absolute. It attacks bourgeois militarism and the bourgeois army, but it is in favour of a revolutionary army of the people.

12. We must enter into a dialogue with young people even though they are idealistic and inexperienced. We must convince them that the army experience is a good training for life.

13. We must intensify our struggle against subversion, which is now appearing in the army in the form of conscientious objection, insubordination, and laziness. Examples will have to be made out of some people, if we are to put order into the ranks.

14. The prominence of the army, and its internal structure, reflect the internal contradictions within the capitalist system of production.

15. Military service, as presently conceived, does not develop the personality but crushes it. Reforms are vital.

16. At the present time our most dangerous enemy is at home, that is to say, left-wing subversion, which is threatening law and order and security.

17. Every military organization within the bourgeois state is a potential vehicle for fascism.

18. We must struggle, using all democratic means, to make sure that the army does not intervene to limit our political rights and freedom of expression.

19. Military training is a way of forcing us to submit to the military hierarchy. It is also a way of training workers and apprentices into unconditional surrender in the factories.

20. Our army has intervened too often against the Swiss workers' movement. We could only trust it now if solid juridical and constitutional guarantees were given.

21. It is a pity that military service does not develop a sense of responsibility and individual liberty but instead moulds individuals into submission under a crushing weight of hierarchy.

22. The army is the institutionalization of the violence within the capitalist state. It is the clear image of the violence implicit in social relations, but camouflaged by bourgeois ideology.

23. The only people who refuse to do their military service are a well-known type— long-haired addicts of drugs and eastern religions who have been taken in by foreign propaganda.

24. The Swiss army has already fired on workers several times. We should keep in mind that they will do so again at the first opportunity—the proof is that they are in active training.

---

[a] The item categories are as follows:
Right-wing: 2, 4, 10, 12, 13, 16, 23.
Moderate: 1, 8, 9, 15, 18, 20, 21.
Left-wing: 3, 5, 6, 7, 11, 14, 17, 19, 22, 24.

(b) The experimental phase

After responding for the first time to the questionnaire, the subjects formed the audience for a ten-minute talk given by a bearded, long-haired confederate who was introduced as belonging to an extreme left-wing anti-militarist group (and therefore wishing to remain anonymous). Consistency in the minority position (opposition to power and specifically to power's repressive military apparatus) was held constant across the two experimental situations (flexible and rigid). The main body of the talk was essentially the same (Mugny, 1974). It was made up of three main sections: the first pointed out the obvious economic support which the army affords to the nation's bourgeoisie; the second denounced the army as an agent of ideological recruitment and reinforcement of the hierarchy underpinning the capitalist division of labour; the last section showed, using historical examples, how the army's essential function is not to defend frontiers but to repress popular and progressive struggles. The vocabulary was derived from anti-militaristic texts of the extreme left, which were widely available at the time.

(c) Rigidity and flexibility in ideological negotiation

We have already pointed out that, in this situation, the negotiation which takes place is in fact anticipatory. We already knew that our subjects favoured conscientious objection as a means of opposition to militarism. Therefore we used this point as the focus for negotiation. Rigid negotiation consisted in harshly criticizing conscientious objection as a means of dissent, whereas flexible negotiation sought to minimize conflict over this issue. In both cases, it is important to note, minority consistency was the same (the more so as the questionnaire was not focussed on the aims of the struggle, but on opinions about the army).

The experimental manipulation, then, was as follows: after the first section of his talk, the confederate paused and then outlined the stance of his group toward conscientious objection: "To weaken the army, we think that revolutionary actions both inside and outside the army are the only effective way; for instance, we think that conscientious objection as a method is too individualistic." He then continued with the second paragraph. This part of the procedure was the same in both experimental conditions.

After the second paragraph, however, the confederate returned to the same point, but in a different manner according to the condition. In the flexible condition, he qualified his stance without contradicting what he had said previously: "*I would like to come back to the point about conscientious objection, which I didn't make very well before. We think that conscientious objection, if it is organized and carried out collectively, is a good and useful means of struggle against the army. I just wanted to say that we think it is important to struggle also from inside the army itself.*" This was done rather as if the speaker had realized that the audience had disapproved of what he had said and as if he had therefore wanted to make a gesture of conciliation.

In the rigid condition, in contrast, at this point the speaker further underlined his criticism of conscientious objection: "*In the struggle against ideological recruitment, we think that methods such as conscientious objection are false, individualistic, petit-bourgeois and quasi-reactionary. To repeat: the struggle must take place both inside and outside the army.*" This hardly needs further comment.

After the talk, the subjects again filled in the questionnaire on attitudes to the army, and then filled in another questionnaire about the image of the minority (cf. Table 3). Finally, they were asked a few supplementary questions, and the session ended with a debriefing.

(d) Results

A straight comparison between the overall levels of influence apparent in each condition, even if the flexible condition reveals greater influence, is not necessarily informative. For this reason, we give separately (Table 8) the means for the pro-militarist, moderate, and anti-militarist item categories. The means represent movement along the 7-point scale between pre- and post-test; on the anti-militarist items, influence is positive if they are shifted leftward on post-test, while the reverse is true for the other two types of item. In the table, + represents positive influence and − represents negative influence.

It will be seen that there is little change on the pro-militarist items; in particular, there is no difference between experimental conditions ($t = 0.477$; *d.f.* 37). This suggests that the subjects already had clear notions with regard to the reactionary character of the militarist position. Indeed, Deconchy (1971) has proposed that it is easier to reject what must be denied (here, militarism) than it is to accept what must be affirmed (but which anti-militarist position here?).

The situation is clearer with the anti-militarist items. Although the difference between conditions is not great ($t = 1.451$, *d.f.* 37: $P < .10$), it is in the predicted direction, since rigid negotiation brings about less change than flexible negotiation. Overall, it is possible to conclude that the subjects did not react unfavourably to the minority position.

However, it does not follow that there has been a simple, positive influence. The results for the moderate items must qualify such a conclusion, since the influence on these items is negative in both conditions, and significantly more so in the rigid condition ($t = 1.698$, *d.f.* 37; one-tailed $P < .05$). In other words, the subjects have judged the

TABLE 8
Mean influence of the minority's speech on the different item categories

	Pro-militarist	Moderate	Anti-militarist
Flexible minority ($n = 20$)	+0.12	−0.14	+0.46
Rigid minority ($n = 19$)	+0.21	−0.59	+0.18

moderate items less "severely" (i.e. as being less to the right), while there is no doubt whatsoever that the minority position entailed that these items should be strongly rejected. Evidently the subjects did not view matters in this light: what they seem to have done, especially in the rigid condition, is to have made a single division of opinions about the army, namely those totally for it (and denounced by the minority), and the rest! This seems to have occurred because the rigid minority led subjects to shift the moderate items less to the right (or more to the left) than it led them to shift the anti-militarist items to the left; *the result is a reduction in the distance between the moderate and the anti-militarist positions.* In contrast, this distance has been increased in the flexible condition, since the anti-militarist items are shifted more to the left than the moderate items.

It is not possible, then, to obtain a simple index of influence by look-ing at the items in an additive fashion. Depending on the style of negotiation, the distribution of opinions is organized in one of two ways: either in a bi-polar distribution (a right/non-right polarity in the rigid condition) or in a more differentiated spread in which there is as much differentiation among the non-right as among the right items, as in the flexible condition. The effects of flexible and rigid negotiation are not, then, directly comparable in a simple quantitative fashion. Greater or lesser influence arises from a complex re-organization of representations. This point should be kept in mind.

(e) The image of the minority

Table 9 gives the evaluation scores for the dimension consistent/inconsistent and flexible/rigid, as well as the correlations between them, for both experimental conditions.

The analysis of these evaluative scores showed that the flexible minority obtained higher scores than the rigid minority. For the flexi-

TABLE 9
Image of the minority

	Consistency/inconsistency	Flexibility/rigidity	Correlation
Flexible minority ($n = 20$)	+3·90	+3·20	+0·15
Rigid minority ($n = 19$)	+2·15	+1·35	+0·63

bility/rigidity dimension this difference is significant ($t = 2 \cdot 049$, $d.f.$ 37; one-tailed $P < \cdot 025$), while for the consistency dimension the difference misses significance ($t = 1 \cdot 626$, $d.f.$ 37; one-tailed $P < \cdot 10$). Thus, not only is rigidity in minority behaviour perceived as such, but it also tends to affect the perception of consistency, since this tends to be noticed more in the flexible condition. This is shown also in the correlation between the scores on the two dimensions: it is low in the flexible condition ($r^{BP} = +0 \cdot 15$; Bravais-Pearson correlation), but significant in the rigid condition ($r^{BP} = +0 \cdot 63$, $P < \cdot 01$). In other words, the more subjects perceived rigidity (and gave a low score on the flexibility/rigidity dimension), the less they noticed consistency (and gave an equally low score on the consistency/inconsistency dimension). By making their rigidity conspicuous, minorities diminish the salience of their consistency, the importance of which in determining the extent of influence we have already seen. Yet there is more to this picture.

One of the questions in the post-experimental interview was to rate the dogmatism of the minority on a 7-point scale from 1 (dogmatic) to 7 (not dogmatic). While 13 out of the 20 subjects in the flexible condition gave a rating of 5 or more and thus rejected the attribution of dogmatism, only 5 out of the 19 subjects in the rigid condition did so; this difference is significant ($\chi^2 = 4 \cdot 413$, one-tailed $P < \cdot 05$).

The rigid minority, then, is not only perceived as such, but this perception tends to affect in turn the perception of consistency and even brings about a categorization of the minority as dogmatic. In a later chapter, we shall see the very great effects these perception processes can have on the ability of minorities to influence.

Experiment 3: Extension to the pollution paradigm

Experiment 3 marks a turning-point in our approach. We used a new paradigm, which we retained for a whole series of experiments. We shall not describe it here in detail (see Chapter 3) except to recapitulate the main points.

First of all, there was no reciprocal interaction between minority and population: the subjects were given texts to read. The procedure was therefore extremely simple, and this allowed us to proceed more rapidly with the series of experiments. The population were school students who took part in the experiments within the school setting.

The procedure consisted of a pre-test, during which subjects filled in a questionnaire about the attribution of responsibility for pollution; followed by the experimental phase, in which they read a text which was either flexible or rigid, and finally there was a post-test, in which the same pre-test questionnaire was filled in again, together with another questionnaire about the image of the minority source.

In this experiment, it will be recalled that influence was evaluated separately for *direct* items, which were verbatim sections of the text, and *indirect* items, which were not part of the text and expressed positions opposed to that of the text. The text strongly condemned industry as being responsible for pollution, while totally rejecting the notion that social categories such as householders and motorists could be responsible. The rigid text included slogans which were so extreme that they would be difficult for subjects to accept, and certainly more so than the flexible slogans.

Let us see, then, whether effects were found similar to those already reported for the first two experiments.

RESULTS

The changes in opinion toward the *direct* and *indirect* items are given in Table 10. An analysis of variance on these results showed that there is no difference between the two conditions in the overall degree of influence exerted ($F = 0.387$, $d.f.$ 1/48). As in the preceding experiment, but with quite different material, we find that it is the *nature* of the changes which is affected by flexibility. In fact, flexibility brings about the same level of influence, regardless of the type of item ($F = 0.004$, $d.f.$ 1/48). In contrast, the rigid minority brings about strongly differentiated effects according to the type of item: it has no effect on the *direct* items but a strong effect on the *indirect* items ($F = 11.912$, $d.f.$ 1/48, $P < .005$). How can these results be interpreted?

TABLE 10
Mean opinion change ($n = 25$)

	Direct	Indirect
Flexible minority	+0.44	+0.43
Rigid minority	−0.11	+0.76

Anticipating later illustration somewhat, we may suppose that changes of opinion bring about a redefinition of a subject's psychosocial identity: this is clearest in respect of the *items*, since to accept them would mean making an explicit move toward the minority's position. When the latter is rigid, this sets up a severe conflict. For reasons discussed earlier, it is difficult for such a subject to move toward a minority which holds an opposed position and with which identification is possible. For a subject confronted with a negotiating minority, the conflict is less, and influence can therefore be more easily acknowledged.

Because the conflict generated by the flexible minority is less, it is easy to understand that, in this condition, influence will be the same on both *direct* and *indirect* items. But why should there be such a marked access of influence on the *indirect* items by the rigid minority? It should be recalled that, in this case, the conflict is particularly intense, and that the subjects have not been willing to resolve it by moving toward the minority on the *direct* items. By accepting minority influence on the items which do not call into question their psychosocial identity, subjects may be attempting to deal with the persistence of this intense conflict. It should be emphasized, however, that the restructuring of opinions is the sign of an underlying chain of inference. We have already seen this in the preceding experiment.

The analogy with the preceding experiment does not stop here: in fact the same reasoning is applicable in both cases. Before we pointed out Deconchy's observation that it seems harder to accept what has to be the case, than to deny what cannot be the case. Now, if we recall that the *indirect* items blame social categories while excusing industry, we see that these are two positions which would both be rejected by the minority—the minority attitude toward these two positions is, moreover, easily inferred. When there is a strong conflict, in which the minority is behaving rigidly, the population may be strongly convinced that certain positions must be rejected, without however accepting the totality of the minority's stance. We will re-encounter this mode of response throughout the experiments to come.

IMAGE OF THE MINORITY

Do we find, at this level also, effects similar to those in the preceding experiment? Table 11 gives the mean evaluation scores for the dimensions of consistency and flexibility/rigidity.

TABLE 11

Evaluation scores (means) for the degree of consistency and of flexibility/rigidity
(n = 25)

	Consistency	Flexibility/rigidity
Flexible minority	+3·40	+1·24
Rigid minority	+3·20	−0·32

Two important points emerge from these results: first, there is no difference between the two experimental conditions in the degree of perceived consistency ($F = 0·101$, $d.f.$ 1/48). It would seem, then, that we have attained a good level of control over the dimension of consistency, essentially because the two texts present the same minority position with the same degree of coherence. It should be recalled that, for our theory, it is important to be able to separate this dimension from that of flexibility/rigidity of negotiation.

With regard to the latter dimension, in contrast, a large difference was apparent, and furthermore in the predicted direction ($F = 6·115$, $d.f.$ 1/48; $P < 0·25$). The experimentally induced rigidity was therefore easily perceived, as well as the relative flexibility in the other condition.

There is a coherence, then, in the effects of this experiment at the two levels of influence and of image of the minority. This coherence makes it possible to explain them at a first level of explanation. For the moment, we will attempt to explain them at the level of the nature of intrasituational relations.

Conclusions

We have defined flexibility and rigidity in negotiation by the degree of polarization of certain positions held by the minority; in other words, by the degree of conflict which the minority arouses in a population which never, as we have seen, totally shares its viewpoint, even though it may not be totally opposed to it. This was the case in the last two experiments, in which the minority polarized very strongly certain positions which were in fact already partially shared by the population studied.

The minority, then, creates a conflict in its relationship with the population. How does the population go about resolving this conflict?

When the minority is flexible and in effect moderates this conflict, the population is able, without too much difficulty, to move toward the minority on certain points, whether these are points which the minority explicitly affirms or implicitly rejects. When the minority is rigid and asserts positions which go "brutally" against the ideological preconceptions of the population, a double effect appears: in general, the population refuses to move toward the points which the minority affirms, while it will yield as far as rejecting, very strongly, points which the minority implicitly rejects.

Moscovici (1980) has already demonstrated that, when confronted with a minority, subjects are reluctant to negotiate openly but that this "counter-blocking" by subjects implies a centring on the object of judgement which leads eventually to a questioning of the dominant mode of judgement. This is clearly what has happened in our experiments, since, in the process of rejecting it, subjects were clearly defining the dominant position, yet without conceding any ground to the minority position. We have also seen that this only seems to be true of a rigid minority showing great intransigence toward the population.

But are matters as simple as this? Can the flexibility of a style be defined in such terms alone? We shall return to this question in the next chapter, when we report the results of modifying some interrelational aspects of situations.

Finally, our measures of the image of the minority have confirmed that the styles we have studied do have consequences at this level. The dimension concerned with the blockage of negotiation (flexibility/ rigidity) is a discriminant, since the flexible minority receives higher scores on this dimension than the rigid minority. The consistency dimension may also be somewhat "contaminated" by negotiating style, as for instance in Experiment 2, in which interindividual conflict was particularly salient. These are certainly strong indications that the perception of the minority may be an important intervening variable. Chapter 6 will report experiments dealing directly with the question of how the minority is perceived, so we shall leave the discussion at this point, except to recall that when a minority is perceived as rigid it may also be categorized as dogmatic.

5

Intrasituational variations in the effects of negotiation

The preceding chapter has shown the effects of various manipulations in the style adopted by a minority in interaction with a population. We have seen that a flexible style had a homogeneous effect on opinion items, whereas a rigid style blocked movement on items explicitly reflecting the minority's position yet produced a greater degree of movement than the flexible style on items which were implicitly (by inference) rejected by the minority position.

The next two experiments set up different relationships between the minority and the population in order to observe their effects on negotiation. Experiment 4 induced subjects to believe that they were either initially in agreement, or in disagreement, with the minority. Experiment 5 made explicit the minority's intention to influence the subjects.

Experiment 4: Negotiation and the aggravation of conflict

Experiment 4 addresses, in one sense, the effect of the distance between influence source and influence receiver. This has been found to be a major variable in influence processes, and models were proposed very early in the history of social psychology to account for it. According to some models, the greater the distance, the less the probability of influence occurring. Other models, conversely, suggested that if conflict were increased, particularly by increasing the distance between parties, the chances of influence occurring would be greater. Common sense then suggested a compromise between these two types of model and proposed that there is an optimal distance, at which influence is maximal; either side of this optimum, influence diminishes as a function of distance. This is recognizably an assimilation and contrast type of model. Suppose that we have an anchor point on a scale of judgement. If assimilation is in fact occurring, it is easy to see that subjects will displace their judgements more if they are already initially displaced from the anchor point. Beyond this, there is a contrast effect, which will be greater as the distance increases. The only problem is to determine the parameters which will allow the precise specification of the anchor point and the latitude of assimilation (or the latitude of rejection).

There is no point in mentioning here the criticisms which have been made of this theory, because there are certain conditions in which its usefulness is beyond doubt. Nemeth and Endicott (1976) have proposed a way of making the model more precise. Their point of departure is that the mid-point of a scale *may* constitute an anchor point, in so far as it is the boundary between two fields of representation: thus, for example, before the mid-point one is for a position; after the mid-point one is against it. Their reasoning is as follows: subjects place themselves at some distance on either side of this scale (they are either for or against); the effect of distance will be different according to whether the minority position (though possibly at the same distance in terms of scale points) is on the same side as, or on the other side from, the subject. In the first case (same side), the influence of the minority should increase with distance, but this will not be true in the second case.

This model allows us to account for the greater effect of rigidity on *indirect* items. We have seen that, on pre-test, subjects were more likely to accept items from all categories than to reject them (scores between 3 and 3·5 on the 7-point scale). In other words, subjects were in agreement with the position stated by the minority (in blaming industry while excusing social categories). However, distance increased on the *indirect* items (which blamed social categories and excused industry) since subjects could infer that these items would be rejected absolutely by the minority (although the subjects tended to be in agreement with them). If we have a sufficient degree of initial agreement between the population and the minority and therefore the population considers that the minority is *on the same side as itself* (*direct* items), we may expect that if the distance between the minority and the population is increased on certain items (*indirect*), minority influence should also increase. Of course this will only hold as long as the minority position on the *indirect* items does not fall beyond the zone of assimilation.

This appears to have been demonstrated in Experiment 3, using the pollution paradigm. Rigidity increased the distance separating the minority and the population by putting forward solutions which the subjects could not easily assent to (the minority pushed the consequences of its analysis to an extreme: if industrial production is responsible for pollution, stop industrial production). The effect of this was, as we have seen, for a rigid style to have more influence on *indirect* items, precisely where the distance between source and receiver was greatest initially, while its influence on the *direct* items was nil, even negative.

This analysis holds as long as we assume that the population and the minority agree in principle on certain positions. If we induce the population to believe that they are in agreement with the minority, we should be able to replicate the effects of Experiment 3. What should we expect to find if a belief in disagreement is induced instead? Will the same effect be exaggerated, or will there be a complete break from the minority (as we saw in the first two experiments with a reactionary minority) because minority positions are then perceived as being within the "latitude of rejection", to revert to the terms of the theory described above? Since we were not in a position to identify the relevant parameters *a priori*, we did not set up a precise hypothesis but awaited the outcome of the experiment.

THE EXPERIMENT (MUGNY AND PAPASTAMOU, 1975–1976)

The pollution paradigm was used once again, with flexible and rigid positions represented by texts. The subjects were induced to believe that they were either in agreement or disagreement with the minority, the latter belief being expected to aggravate minority/population conflict, since it calls to attention the distance between them.

(a) Experimental manipulations

During pre-test, subjects filled in the usual opinion questionnaire. Following this, the experimenter announced that their responses would be examined by a group of research workers engaged in a study of the environment and would be categorized according to whether or not they were in agreement with the position of this group. To assure anonymity a coding system was used, and this added to the plausibility of the situation.

During the week separating the pre-test from the remaining two phases of the experiment, the responses of the 112 subjects were examined and used to determine the allocation of subjects to experimental groups. The subjects were distributed at random over four experimental conditions, with the restriction that any large differences arising between groups were corrected.

The agreement/disagreement manipulation was introduced at the beginning of the experimental phase. Subjects each individually received a letter (reproduced in Table 12), in which the influence source stated whether the subject's questionnaire responses had been in agreement with the environmental research group's position. Half the subjects received a letter indicating that they were in agreement with the group, and half received one indicating that they were in disagreement. The subjects next received a text which explained the group's own position: half the subjects in each agreement/disagree-

TABLE 12
Letter received by subjects indicating agreement or disagreement (variation in italics and bracketed) between source and receiver

---

Dear

CODE NO.

We have read very carefully your answers to the pollution opinion questionnaire distributed by OPRG.[a] We are writing to you to let you know that we are in complete (*dis*)agreement with your point of view on this issue.

A detailed analysis of your answers has indicated that there is a (*wide divergence*) close convergence between your opinion and ours.

We have accordingly classified you, according to your answers, in the group of persons "in (*dis*)agreement with us".

Since we are (*not*) in agreement, we thought it would be helpful to let you know our own complete position, which you will find in the enclosed letter.

Yours sincerely

Environmental Research Group

PS   We have replied to your Code no., in strict observance of your anonymity.

---

[a] The experimenters introduced themselves as members of an Opinion-Poll Research Group.

ment condition received a flexible text, and half received a rigid text.

Finally, subjects filled in the pre-test questionnaire once more, and also a questionnaire concerning their image of the influence source.

(b) Results

Table 13 gives the mean values for opinion changes on the *direct* and *indirect* items, for each of the four experimental conditions.

The results indicate a significant interaction among the three variables ($F = 9\cdot200$, *d.f.* 1/108; $P < \cdot005$). In attempting to interpret this result, it is interesting first of all to notice that in the agreement situation the pattern of results is the same as that seen in Experiment 3. The flexible minority has the same degree of influence on both types of item, whereas the rigid minority has little influence on the *direct* items, but has much more (causing a shift of more than one point along a 7-point scale) on the *indirect* ones (interaction: $F = 8\cdot005$ *d.f.* 1/108; $P < \cdot01$). We can therefore suppose that there was initial relative agreement, in principle, between the subjects and the minority source, since the induction of agreement did not change the pattern of responses.

However, the situation is quite different when disagreement is induced between the subjects and the minority. The results indicate that we were successful in manipulating the intensity of the minority/population conflict by emphasizing (by means of the brutally explicit letter) the disagreement between the subject's responses and the position put forward in the text. In this disagreement situation, the flexible text had, as expected, a strong influence on the *direct* items, an effect which seems to arise from other mechanisms. Yet there was also a very great increment of influence on the *indirect* items ($F = 11\cdot387$, *d.f.* 1/108; $P < \cdot01$), an effect as great as that obtained on indirect

TABLE 13
Mean opinion changes ($n = 28$)

	Agreement		Disagreement	
	Direct	Indirect	Direct	Indirect
Flexible minority	+0·51	+0·57	+0·48	+1·30
Rigid minority	+0·11	+1·14	+0·20	+0·52

items by the rigid minority in an agreement situation. It is possible to
conclude that *flexibility in negotiation is more effective in proportion as the
minority/population conflict is explicit and severe*; this is a clear illustration of
our theory.

In contrast, the limits on the possibilities of rigid negotiation
become apparent when conflict, already severe due to the rigidity
itself, is aggravated by inducing explicit disagreement. Although there
is no change in the degree of influence on *direct* items (thus confirming
that this involves a different process, to be considered later), the *indirect* items are much less influenced in comparison to the agreement
condition ($F = 6.664$, *d.f.* 1/108; $P < .025$). The increment of conflict
appears to have severely limited the persuasive power of the rigid
source. When minority/population conflict is too sharply felt, rigidity
brings about a counter-blockage to negotiation by the subjects themselves. Here is the beginning of alienation, at all levels, which goes
some way to explain why, in our first two experiments, a rigid minority had less influence than a flexible minority on items which could
also be described as being *indirect*. In these cases, it should be recalled,
the minority was present in person, and the conflict was particularly
felt. The pollution paradigm appears, in itself, to be a less conflict-
evoking topic: it is relatively mundane, which incidentally made it
suitable for the school setting in a way that the first two experiments
were clearly not. At the same time, this paradigm had the undoubted
advantage that the conflict created, although not shocking to the subjects, who were already somewhat in agreement with the minority
position, was sufficiently strong to make the effects of rigidity felt.
Thus, the conflict was strong enough to be definitely a factor, yet not so
strong as to impede influence effects from occurring. We appear to
have located a border-line zone between acceptance and rejection,
where the nature of our manipulations may reverse effects, sometimes
causing acceptance and sometimes rejection of the minority position.

Finally, we come to the image of the minority formed during the
course of this experiment. The effects were in fact too slight to be worth
reporting in detail. The agreement condition brought about a higher
score of judged flexibility than the disagreement condition (thus confirming that the disagreement condition did indeed bring about conflict). In both conditions, the rigid text was judged to emanate from a
very slightly less flexible source. Why were these effects so slight? It is
possible that the measuring instrument itself was not sufficiently sen-

sitive. It is also possible that the interaction between influence and image is extremely complex; since the latter was assessed after the subjects had answered the opinion questionnaire for the second time, it could be that the fact of having changed their responses made them less willing to give expression to the conflict they may have felt. It may not always be easy to make a negative judgement of a source which has, after all, convinced us a little.

The image of the source was only a supplementary measure in this particular experiment. To have a clearer understanding of the effect of the image of the source, it is necessary to manipulate it directly, as an independent variable. This is done in the next chapter.

Experiment 5: Rigidity and the intention to influence

Does the rigid minority, through its intransigence, give the impression that it has the intention to influence? To refuse to cede could, in effect, signify that since it will not allow itself to be influenced, the intention must be to impose its own position on the population. This reasoning could be said to follow, also, from the theory of reactance developed by Brehm (1966) and later Wicklund (1974) to account for social influence.

The theory of reactance is extremely simple: if an individual has consciousness of the power to make one choice amongst others, hence of freedom, then any event which either eliminates one of these possibilities, or threatens to eliminate it, creates a state of reactance. Reactance is a motivational state directed toward the recovery of lost or threatened liberty. Extended to the question of social influence, this theory would predict that if we perceive an influence source as having the intention to influence, we shall tend to reject the source, because it threatens our freedom to choose an opinion. In Lewinian terms, we would be caught between two forces: one pressing toward conformity with the source, and the other toward retention of autonomy of judgement.

This theory would offer an attractive interpretation of the negative effects of rigidity, if it were not for the apparently contradictory effects of a rigid minority,* that is, its lack of influence on *direct* items,

---

* Brehm and Mann (1975) happen to have found a similar effect, though they do not attempt to explain it.

together with an often strong influence on *indirect* items (in conditions where, as we have just seen, the intensity of conflict does not pass a certain threshold of outright rejection).

We have proposed elsewhere (Mugny and Doise, 1979) a more systematic critique of the theory of reactance. Nevertheless, this theory has suggested to us an experiment which helps clarify the mechanisms which could be involved in the effects of rigidity.

The experiment is based on a very simple principle. We informed the subjects that the intention of the authors of the text was to persuade them and that our study was designed to measure their success in achieving this. This gave us the possibility of creating an eventual state of reactance. However, we part company from the theory of reactance in the nature of our predictions. Essentially, the theory predicts that reactance is stronger as persuasive pressure increases. Thus, if one were to say to certain subjects that the source was interested only in influencing them, reactance should be stronger than in subjects who were given to believe that the source was interested in their own opinions as well and was taking these into account. The theory would predict greater influence in the second case.

Our predictions are different. We know that the effects of rigidity are different according to the nature of the items (*direct* or *indirect*). Rigidity has this dual effect because it induces strong conflict (at least, stronger conflict than that induced by flexibility). Furthermore, the subjects are in a situation in which they know it is impossible for them to have any effect on the source. Because of the experimental situation, influence is one-way only, and there can be no direct interaction between the subjects and the influence source. But what if we suddenly told the subjects that they in turn had the opportunity to influence the source, that they were in real interaction with the source, even though through the intermediary of the experimenter? The presence of the source, even if only symbolic, should make rigidity more salient, since the minority/population relationship is thus brought home very directly to the subjects.

THE EXPERIMENT

Again we used the pollution paradigm, with the usual pre-test and post-test questionnaire.

(a) Experimental manipulations

There were four experimental conditions, focussing on the effects of rigidity: three used a rigid text, and the fourth used a flexible one.

In the first two conditions, either a rigid or a flexible text was used. Each text was accompanied by an explanation stating that the source who had produced the text was interested only in how far it was capable of influencing a given population, and in nothing more. The subjects were told to read the text and afterwards fill in the same opinion questionnaire as before, in order to see how far they had changed. In a machiavellian sense, one could say, we had told these subjects the "truth". We called these two conditions "unilateral" because there was only one possible direction of influence. If our characterization of this situation is correct and the subjects had no expectation whatsoever of being able to affect the minority's position, we should expect to find the "usual" effects of flexibility and rigidity.

The control condition used a rigid text and simply informed subjects that we wanted to see how much influence the text would have on people, without attributing any particular intention to the source.

The remaining condition also used a rigid text and also informed subjects that the source was interested in the effect of the text on a given population. However, this was the "reciprocal" influence condition; subjects were told in addition that the source was interested in the population's opinions and would take account of them in producing a more definitive text which would better represent public opinion in general. The subjects could therefore take an active role, and even expect to have an effect, however slight, on the whole population. But at the same time the reciprocal relationship between the minority and the population became salient, and its accompanying conflict. We hypothesized that the conflict would therefore be felt as exacerbated.

(b) Results

To begin with, we shall consider the image of the minority source. Once again, only weak effects occurred. Nevertheless, they suggest that our manipulation had the intended effect, since rigidity was most felt in the rigid condition with reciprocal influence. When the subjects saw that a return influence was possible (their opinions were taken into account) yet that the text, because of its rigidity, in fact ruled out any possibility of conciliation between them and the minority, conflict was at its maximum (contrary to the prediction which would be made by the theory of reactance, incidentally). What were the influence effects? Table 14 gives the influence means for *direct* and *indirect* items in the four conditions.

As the preceding experiments would have led us to expect, there is a strong interaction between the type of item and the experimental variation: $F = 6\cdot487$, *d.f.* 2/57; $P < \cdot005$ (excluding the control condition).

We also expected the two unilateral conditions to bring about the usual effects of flexibility and rigidity. Although this time the flexible source appears to have had a different effect on *direct* and *indirect* items, suggesting that the situation this time was more conflictual than previous ones, in fact the difference between the item types is not significant ($F = 1\cdot301$, *d.f.* 1/57) whereas in the rigid text condition this difference is highly significant ($F = 8\cdot054$, *d.f.* 1/57; $P < \cdot01$). Since the expected pattern has been partly reproduced, we may conclude that the subjects had a realistic appraisal of the experimental situation. They must have perceived it as constricting and unilateral: even when its unilateral nature was made explicit in the stated intention to influence, the same effects occurred! On the other hand, rigidity had the same effect when unilaterality was not attributed to the source but was apparent in that the experimenters' interest was merely in the effect of the text. Thus, when the intention to influence is held constant, ideological negotiation has its own characteristic effect. At any rate, an explanation solely in terms of intention to influence is clearly not sufficient. This is shown further by the effects of the rigid condition which held out the promise of reciprocity: instead of reducing conflict, this actually increased it. Not only was rigidity somewhat more perceptible by the subjects, but the usual effects of rigidity were accentuated: there was no change at all on the *direct* items (considering

TABLE 14

Mean opinion changes ($n = 20$)

	Direct	Indirect
Flexible minority, unilateral	+0·48	+0·74
Rigid minority, unilateral	+0·19	+0·83
Rigid minority (control)	+0·23	+0·97
Rigid minority, reciprocal	−0·08	+1·30

the mean value, of course) while the effect on the *indirect* items reached a maximum ($F = 37.808$, *d.f.* $1/57$; $P < .0005$).

A few final remarks before leaving the theory of reactance. Suppose (and we say "suppose" advisedly) that this theory had been able to predict that the disappointed hope of reciprocity brought about by rigidity would lead to the perception of a stronger threat! This theory would then be able to explain only half of the effects obtained, namely those on the *direct* items, which underwent less change as a function of the perception of minority blocking of negotiation. It could not explain the greater influence on the *indirect* items.

Conclusions

The two experiments reported in this chapter have hardly led to any theoretical advance. Nevertheless, they allowed us to confirm the nature of the effects produced by flexible and rigid minorities and to understand something of the conditions in which these effects may or may not occur.

First, there has been a double confirmation: the text putting forward a flexible minority position *tends* to have a relatively homogeneous influence on *direct* and *indirect* items, while the introduction of rigidity *tends* to block the appearance of influence on *direct* items, but in parallel to increase (relative to flexibility) the access of influence on *indirect* items. Our initial interpretation of the different effects of rigidity and flexibility is that rigidity brings about a stronger conflict in the minority/population relationship than flexibility does. For reasons that subsequent chapters will clarify, this conflict prevents subjects from ceding on the items which directly express the minority position with which they are in disagreement. Nevertheless, the conflict is sufficiently great to cause subjects to question themselves about the alternative proposed and to modify certain of their responses. In effect, they appear to allow themselves to be convinced about the items they can infer that the minority reject. Thus, they reject more forcefully than in a flexible condition those propositions which we have considered to be dominant in the overall social system, but they are less willing to ally themselves with a minority position which puts their initial opinions more brutally in question.

This apparently paradoxical effect depends not only on the nature of the source's ideological stance (flexible or rigid) but also on the relationship between the minority and the population. The two experiments in this chapter have shown that the same effects appear when an agreement between the minority and the population is emphasized and even when the unilateral character of the influence relationship is pointed out to subjects. In other words (as we indicated in our initial description of the paradigm) relative agreement already exists between the minority and the subjects on certain propositions. Further, these effects also occur in the case where subjects appear to accept the one-way nature of the relationship.

Yet there is more. The effects of flexibility and rigidity are especially divergent when the situation is such that the conflictual aspect of the minority/population relationship is emphasized. First of all, the flexible minority, without losing any of its persuasiveness on *direct* items, also convinces subjects, to a greater degree, that they should reject the dominant propositions expressed in the *indirect* items. In this situation, negotiation appears to be a necessity imposed by the extreme opposition between minority and population. In a situation which is essentially similar, the influence of a rigid minority is reduced even on *indirect* items, where it has otherwise greatest effect.

The effect of rigidity, then, is modulated according to the expectations that subjects are given: when subjects expect a reciprocal relationship in which they may be able to have some influence on the minority, the effects of rigidity are accentuated. Subjects' expectations that they may have some effect on the minority's own position seem to be an important variable in these effects.

In these first experiments on the effects of negotiation styles, we have attempted to gain some idea of the image of the minority influence source held by subjects. We did this by using a questionnaire instrument, but the results of this have been disappointing. The results have often been in the predicted direction: the perception of consistency tends not to differ according to whether the condition is flexible or rigid (except when conflict is particularly salient); whereas flexibility is much more likely to be perceived, not surprisingly, in conditions with a flexible text. We have already suggested that the weakness of these results may be explained by interference between the opinion ratings and the questionnaire designed to assess the image of the source, since the latter was responded to *after* the final opinion rating. This sequence was of course adopted in order to avoid interference in the reverse direction.

However, the perception of the source is an essential component of our theory, and therefore it is essential to manipulate this image directly. This is what we attempt to do in the next chapter.

6

Negotiation and perception of the minority: categorization, individualization, and naturalization

The process of negotiation between minority and population plays a vital role, but this process itself takes place, as we have indicated, through the mediation of mechanisms of perception of the minority source. It is perceived consistency which is a necessary factor in minority influence, and it is perceived rigidity which "blocks" the population. However, we must not be seduced by words. As we have seen, there is no such thing as rigidity in isolation, any more than flexibility can exist in isolation. These are only the consequences of situations which lead the population to *interpret* minority behaviours as more or less rigid or flexible. This chapter will be concerned with such interpretations of minority behaviours.

In the preceding experiments, the relative difficulty in grasping the nature of these images of rigidity and flexibility has been apparent. We optimistically describe the difficulty as "relative" because although the results so far obtained have not been systematic, they nevertheless surely indicate the manner in which these representations can be fruitfully studied.

Thus, it is generally true that, in our experiments, the extent of perceived flexibility is greater when the minority is not coercive in its negotiation with the population. Certain results from Experiment 2 are essential to this point; we found significant correlations between the degree of perceived consistency and the degree of flexibility, when the source was rigid. In fact, there was a very slight correlation when the confederate made a flexible speech, but a significant positive correlation when he contradicted the population in a rigid manner. In other words, it is not so much, or at least not only, the content of the minority's image which is important, but rather the organization of the image. Rigidity, when it is perceived (we cannot insist too much on this point: *when it is perceived*) brings about a sort of halo effect. The image will be organized around a central dimension, that relating to negotiation blocking. It is therefore understandable that rigidity can, when conflict is strong, lose all or some of its ability to influence. If consistency is also perceived as well but is associated with the image of the minority as rigid, the negative character of this rigidity will then assimilate the consistency. Even if it is perceived, the consistency will be understood by the population as a simple consequence of minority rigidity.

The perception of a minority as rigid is, in effect, a negative evaluation. This is translated into a categorization of the source in terms of dogmatism, as another result of our second experiment shows. This categorization prevents the population from openly acknowledging minority positions: being dogmatic, the minority will be perceived as having closed its "frontiers" of its own accord, by implying "thus far and no further" and thus rejecting all other positions, those of the population included. There can be no negotiation with such a minority, nor any approach to it no matter how tentative: we have seen that *direct* questionnaire items in a rigidity condition never manifest influence even approaching a level of significance.

However, to take things in their proper order, what we aim to do in this chapter is to make the population's representation of the minority into an independent variable (rather than, as in the preceding experiments, treat it as a measure). By manipulating it as an independent variable, we shall be able to evaluate the grounds of our interim conclusions about the nature of the minority image. To begin at the beginning: rigidity is translated into an image with precise content. It is this which we proceed to vary experimentally.

Experiment 6: Induction of the content of the minority image

The pollution paradigm is used once more as the basis of this experiment. Experiment 6 is similar to Experiment 3 in all respects except one: before the subjects read the flexible version of the text, they received information about how other people before them had perceived the authors of the text. In an induced rigidity condition, we told subjects that people who had read this text before them had judged the authors to be *unfriendly, hard, obstinate, rigid, intolerant, hostile, stubborn, domineering, authoritarian,* and *arrogant.* In other words, we gave them the list of ten adjectives we obtained from our measure of minority-image rigidity (see p. 65). In the induced flexibility condition, we used the "flexible" adjectives: the authors were said to have been perceived by previous readers as *sociable, understanding, tolerant, likeable, realistic, balanced, pleasant, open, cooperative,* and *adaptable.* The subjects were 31 members of a catechism class, who took part in the experiment while at their religious institution. Fifteen were assigned to the induced flexibility condition, and 16 to the induced rigidity condition.

RESULTS

It should first of all be noted that the final measure of the minority image again did not lead to a significant result. In fact the subjects chose to use very few of the adjectives, far fewer than in the other experiments. The post-experimental discussion made it clear that this was because they had felt it very difficult to make choices on the basis of such little information (the text alone), and because they had not wanted to be influenced by the list of adjectives they had received in advance. Did these adjective-lists, emphasising the flexibility or the rigidity of the minority, in fact have any effect on minority influence? Table 15 contains the answer to this question.

When the experimentally induced image of the minority is congruent with the nature of the text, the image has a significant degree of influence. However, when a rigid image is induced of a text which has been hitherto characterized as flexible, the text's influence is diminished ($F = 4\cdot358$, *d.f.* 1/29; $P < \cdot05$). The nature of an alternative position is therefore less important than the perception one is led to have of it, and this in turn depends on various situational factors.

TABLE 15
Mean opinion change

	Direct	Indirect
"Flexible" minority ($n = 15$)	$-0\cdot03$	$+0\cdot54$
"Rigid" minority ($n = 16$)	$-0\cdot21$	$+0\cdot18$

A further finding, which was independent of the experimental conditions, was that the *direct* items manifested less influence than the *indirect* ones ($F = 7.009$, *d.f.* 1/29; $P < .025$). This was expected in the rigid induction condition, since we have found the same effect many times before, but how is it to be explained in the flexible induction condition, when previously we have always found (in the pollution paradigm) that flexibility leads to equal influence on both types of item? Initially, one might be tempted to seek the answer in the religious context in which the experiment took place, but, beyond this situational difference, the subjects were similar to those in the other experiments.

An *a posteriori* answer to this question is both more plausible and allows us to advance theoretically from this point: the effect arises from the manner in which the image was induced. We shall show that causing subjects to focus on psychological characteristics of the minority brings into play certain ideological processes relating to deviance and leads subjects to avoid any possible identification with the source. First, however, we shall see how it is possible to modify the content of an image by modifying the mode of categorization. For this we turn to an elegant experiment by Ricateau.

Ricateau's experiment: Categorization processes and rigidity

Rigidity can reduce the influence of a minority when this quality is merely induced as part of the content of the minority's image. But this perception of rigidity also appears to have consequences for the internal organization of the whole set of possible dimensions of judgement. Thus, the dimension of consistency, in particular, plays an essential role in minority influence. However, we have already had several indications that, if perceived, rigidity tends to contaminate the perception of consistency, so it would appear to have a central role in the set of representations relative to the minority; it is around this dimension that the others are oriented, and from it they take on their meaning. Thus there appears to be within the population a kind of restriction of the cognitive field, since it is organized around a single dimension which is the most salient in the minority/population relationship: that relating to negotiation-blocking.

Ricateau's experiment illustrates this process directly. He "trained" subjects to use varying numbers of judgement categories in their perceptions of the minority. He also demonstrated that the restriction of the cognitive field relative to the perception of minorities extends to the situation in which there is face-to-face contact with the minority and that the result of this is that rigid negotiation-blocking becomes a salient dimension around which the image of the minority is organized, thus weakening its influence.

THE EXPERIMENT (RICATEAU, 1970–1971)

The subjects were psychology students. In groups of three (of whom one was a confederate) they spent half an hour discussing the case of a juvenile delinquent and deciding what would be the appropriate treatment for him. The confederate consistently put forward the most severe recommendation (place the delinquent in a remand home and then send him to prison) and refused to accommodate at all to the experimental subjects, who generally opted for "softer" treatments such as psychiatric supervision. The procedure can be summarized as follows:

(1) The subjects described each other member of the group using 2, 5, or 8 rating scales, each being a 6-point scale specifying characteristics which were not relevant to the interaction, such as active/passive, realist/romantic, etc. The number of scales was the only independent variable. The aim was to induce subjects to use a mode of person-perception which was either relatively monolithic or pluridimensional, i.e. to perceive the other persons using either few or many dimensions. The theoretical justification of this method was that a strongly monolithic categorization should increase the salience or the psychological importance of the most conspicuous information (in the present experiment, this would be negotiation-blocking, the refusal to accommodate, which was the most conspicuous feature of the interindividual conflict created by the confederate's strong dissent).

(2) Individually, the subjects read a passage describing the delinquent's case.

(3) Individually again, the subjects selected a treatment from a scale of 7 possibilities, ranging from an extremely lenient to an extremely harsh one.

(4) Ten minutes' discussion in the groups of 3 (including the con-
     federate, who supported the harshest treatment).
(5) New description of the group members, using 2, 5, or 8 rating
     scales, according to the experimental condition.
(6) Further 10-minute discussion.
(7) Final description of the others using the same 2, 5, or 8 scales.
(8) Final 10-minute discussion.
(9) Assessment of the image of the other group members: subjects
     chose from 100 adjectives to describe each member.
(10) New individual selection of treatment for the delinquent.

The confederate behaved in the same consistent manner in each
group and in each condition, putting forward arguments which had
been pre-arranged for each phase of the discussion to justify a clearly
minority position. In each group, the confederate created strong conflict by behaving in a style that we can call rigid. How much influence
did the confederate have, and how was this achieved in relation to the
number of dimensions the subjects used in perceiving him?

The results supported the author's hypothesis: as the number of rating scales increased, so did the influence of the confederate. We should
recall, however, that this was not a matter of simple submission to the
confederate by the subjects, but rather a matter of compromise: they
displaced their responses on the treatment rating scale by one or more
points, but they never gave the extreme response that was recommended throughout by the confederate.

The mode of categorization imposed by the experimenter affected
the content and the internal organization of the induced image.
Ricateau was able to analyse those of the 100 adjectives actually used
into 6 categories: personality, physical, cognitive, and emotional
characteristics, attitudes, and negotiation-blocking characteristics
related to rigidity. The more rating scales the subjects had at their disposal, the more likely they were to attribute cognitive characteristics
to the minority, and the less likely they were to choose adjectives relating to negotiation-blocking. It is possible to conclude that Ricateau
was manipulating a variable which was at the level of mechanisms
determining minority social influence. In other words, those
mechanisms are to be found at the level of categorization of the influence source.

To return to the question of the effect of rigidity, we can also conclude that in a situation of inter-individual conflict, rigidity renders

certain minority behaviours salient. Intense conflict leads subjects to adopt a rather monolithic image in which the central dimension is negotiation-blocking, and this may reach a stage at which the minority is categorized as dogmatic. To use a gestaltist metaphor, negotiation-blocking creates a figure/ground effect in which the figure is salient to such a degree that the ground is not noticed: rigidity can, in effect, mask the behavioural consistency which we already know to be influential. This masking effect, as we have seen, can be brought about by actual negotiation-blocking behaviours themselves, but it can also be modulated (again when the blocking behaviour is real) by the particular perceptions induced by the experimenter, as our Experiment 6 and Ricateau's experiment show.

It is important to note, however, that in our first experiments we did not explicitly induce any categorizations. Furthermore, the assessment of the minority image which we used, which was suggestive of some of these dimensions, was not carried out until after we had taken the opinion ratings measuring the extent of influence. Since we only manipulated ideological contents in terms of more or less rigidity or flexibility, we must suppose that *the effects of rigidity differed from those of flexibility because each brought about a specific categorization, a dominant mode of perception which explains the regularity of occurrence of the results we have obtained.* The conflict engendered by a rigid position should provide a means for the relevant categorization to be made explicit. If this is true, then, following Ricateau's example, it should be possible to modulate the phenomenon.

Experiment 7: Rigidity and individualization

The two preceding experiments have allowed us to make some advance in explaining the effects of rigidity: by bringing about conflict between the minority and the population, rigidity makes the population sensitive to those behaviours which appear to be the cause of the conflict. The population will therefore focus its attention on negotiation-blocking behaviours, to the detriment of other dimensions. This focus on the population's representation of the minority is clearly shown in Ricateau's experiment which, while holding rigidity constant, varied the number of dimensions used by the population in judging the minority. The fewer the dimensions used, the more rigidity was a central dimension.

But why should this bring about a reduction of influence? After all, not all characteristics of the source are relevant to the case being made. We do not believe what a person says any the less merely because we do not like his face. There must be some reason why the image of the source intervenes in the influence process: the image must have some relevance to the establishment of a new response. Probably, then, the image is related in some way to the alternative position being proposed by the minority. We can then hypothesize that whenever the minority's position is attributed to (or explained by) the image perceived, rigidity will have less influence than flexibility. This will not be the case if the image is not sufficient to explain the behaviour of the minority.

Experiments 7 and 8 illustrate this precondition of the effects of rigidity. Experiment 8 focuses subjects either on the minority's personality (possibly, therefore, on blocking behaviour) or on the content of the communication (thus avoiding reference to the source). Experiment 7, which we will report first, varies the number of minority sources: if several minorities express a similar viewpoint, although they are perceived to be independent, it will be less possible to attribute the minority viewpoint to characteristics of the minorities themselves, as represented in the several image contents.

In effect, what these two experiments attempt to do is to "de-individualize" the minority and hence to diminish the obstacle that blocking behaviours can create to the establishment of new opinions.

THE EXPERIMENT (MUGNY AND PAPASTAMOU, 1980)

Seventy-two subjects were distributed across four conditions. The pollution paradigm was used, with the exception that the assessment of the source image was carried out *before* the second opinion rating, in the hope of obtaining stronger effects.

Half of the subjects received a flexible text, and half received a rigid text. In each condition, the text was attributed to either one or two minority sources. This was done by telling the subjects that we had contacted two fringe minority groups and asked for their responses to the question "who is responsible for pollution?" In the one-minority condition the subjects received the complete text with the exception of the introductory paragraph, which was presented as the question which had been posed to the minority group(s). In the two-minority condition, the text was simply divided into two sections; paragraphs B and C together, and paragraphs D and E together (see the description of experimental material, Chapter 3, Table 2). The first two paragraphs were attributed to a minority "A", and the last two to a minority "B". The order of presentation of the paragraphs and their attribution to the minorities were of course controlled. We ensured that the two fictitious minorities would be perceived as independent by making use of this division into paragraphs in the text, since the content of each paragraph was totally different. The style of the paragraphs was, however, standardized. We explained this by telling the subjects that it was the *content* of the minorities' viewpoint that interested us and to avoid any interference due to the style of the two passages we had rewritten them both in the same style.

(a) Results: the image of the source

What were the effects of one- as compared to two-minority sources on the content of the minority image? Table 16 gives the scores relating to consistency and flexibility. The scores in the two-minority conditions are the means of the scores for each of the two minorities.

The results indicate that one or two flexible minorities obtained a higher score than one or two rigid minorities ($F = 4.309$, *d.f.* 1/68; $P < .05$). This is true for both perceived consistency and perceived flexibility. In this experiment, then, there was overall a more positive evaluation of minority flexibility. Note that we appear to have met the conditions needed to establish a link between image and influence: the number of minorities does not mask the flexibility or rigidity of the positions proposed.

TABLE 16
Image of the minority source(s) ($n = 18$)

	Consistency	Flexibility/rigidity
1 Flexible minority	+5·89	+1·89
1 Rigid minority	+4·00	+0·22
2 Flexible minorities	+4·58	+1·56
2 Rigid minorities	+2·97	−0·19

(b) Results: influence

Table 17 gives the mean influence scores for *direct* and *indirect* items.

There is one general difference which is apparent in all the conditions: the influence on *direct* items is almost nil, or even slightly negative, while it is very strong on the *indirect* items ($F = 43 \cdot 701$, *d.f.* 1/68; $P < \cdot 0005$). Why should this be so? Our previous results had led us to expect that a flexible minority would have equal influence on both types of item. At this point, we offer an *a posteriori* explanation, whose theoretical implications will be made clearer in a later chapter. There is a methodological difference between this experiment and the previous ones: in the previous experiments, we had not explicitly characterized the source in any way but merely let it be believed, by implication, that the positions proposed by the source were unusual within the population as a whole. Thus we did not emphasize the minority identity of the source, and it is possible, at least in the flexible condition, that the subjects were mistaken as to the identity of the source. It is known (see McGuire, 1969) that the non-identification of a source in an experimental situation can lead to perception of the source as highly credible, no doubt by simple association with the authority and prestige of the scientific setting. Rigidity, in contrast, because the behaviour in itself makes apparent the minority character of the position being put forward (as we shall see in detail in Experiment 10), brings about the blocking effect with which we are now familiar. In the present experiment, it may have been sufficient for the experimenter to make explicit reference to the categorial affiliation of the source ("It is a minority") for the conflict felt as a result to be expressed in immediate rejection of minority positions. We shall come back later to this important question, concluding for the moment that a flexible source may be influential to the extent that its minority character is masked.

TABLE 17
Mean opinion changes ($n = 18$)

	Direct	Indirect
1 Flexible minority	+0·15	+0·95
1 Rigid minority	−0·08	+0·38
2 Flexible minorities	−0·01	+0·90
2 Rigid minorities	+0·10	+1·08

Accepting this interpretation for the moment, we go on to point out that there is a significant interaction between the two independent variables ($F = 4.606$, d.f. 1/68; $P < .05$). This is brought about as follows: a single, rigid minority in general has less influence than a single flexible minority ($F = 4.665$, d.f. 1/68; $P < .05$), while two minorities have the same degree of influence whether they are flexible or rigid ($F = 0.766$, d.f. 1/68; not significant).

At first sight, then, our hypotheses appear to be confirmed: it is the unique, or individualized, character of the minority which causes blocking behaviours to be its salient perceived feature. However, the picture is not quite so simple as this: as we have seen, the evaluation of the source (assessment of the image) is equally poor in the case of a rigid minority regardless of whether it is the only source, or one of two. How can these diverse effects be accounted for? Suppose we make our hypothesis more specific and predict that when the source is unique, the image of the source will be relevant to the formation of new opinions, but that when there is more than one source, their images will be less relevant.

(c) Correlations between image and influence

Since we have obtained significant effects on both image and influence in this experiment, we can proceed to look for correlations between them. Using Bravais-Pearson's r, we calculated the corrrelation between the overall image score and the overall influence score (i.e. the overall scores from these two measures which were used to show that the experimental manipulations had a significant effect). The correlations are given in Table 18.

These results are interesting: they show that when there is only a single minority, a link tends to be established between image and

TABLE 18
Correlations between minority influence and minority image

1 Flexible minority	$+0.387$ ($P < 0.10$)
1 Rigid minority	$+0.402$ ($P < 0.05$)
2 Flexible minorities	-0.139
2 Rigid minorities	$+0.119$

influence (flexible minority), significantly so in the case of a rigid minority. Opinion change becomes more likely as flexibility is perceived. Recall that our image assessment showed that a rigid minority is not highly evaluated, so it is not surprising that its influence is less. Nor is it surprising that the addition of another rigid minority to an existing one does not diminish the level of influence, because the image, even if "correctly perceived" by the subjects, does not enter into relation with the influence process.

In other words, characteristics of the image may well determine the explanation which subjects formulate themselves to account for minority behaviours: if the minority holds rigid positions, it is because it is dogmatic, and so on. The image perceived becomes the explanatory cause of alternative, minority behaviours. By experimentally creating two independent minorities, we did not simply diminish perceived rigidity, but we made it difficult (because implausible) for the behaviour of two apparently unrelated minorities to be interpretable in terms of identical characteristics of dogmatism.

This "individualizing" interpretation of the perception of minority positions appears to be general enough to take account of the systematic difficulties which our minorities had, especially the rigid ones, in exerting influence in the first experiments. What was happening in those cases (as we argued in Chapter 3) was that a basic ideological mechanism intervened in the relationship between population and minority, which was explicitly demonstrated in the experimental situations we set up. In the present experiment, because two independent minorities presented the same positions, the activation of this mechanism was prevented. The next experiment also attempts to subvert the logic of this mechanism.

Experiment 8: Rigidity and psychologization

Experiment 7 showed that the effects of rigidity only appear when minority behaviours are interpretable through the image which the minority projects. The population's reasoning would appear to be: "It is because it *is* rigid that the minority defends its positions in such a manner". This reasoning is not invoked when there are two minorities. In other words, individualization of the source appears to be necessary for it to be rejected. This individualization leads the population to attribute the antagonistic relationship which develops between power and the minority (when the minority is consistent) to factors lying outside the relationship itself, namely idiosyncratic characteristics of the minority. However, these imputed characteristics themselves also arise out of the ideological process and are often of a psychological nature, such as tolerance, intolerance, etc. Even when such characteristics can only be expressed within a social relationship, they will still be perceived as belonging intrinsically to the minority. Therefore, if a population are asked to identify the psychological characteristics which underlie minority behaviours, this is tantamount to undermining the innovating alternative the minority may be putting forward, and the minority henceforward is bound to have less influence than if the population had been focused on the content of the minority message. We see this taking place in the eighth experiment.

THE EXPERIMENT (PAPASTAMOU *ET AL.*, 1980)

Eighty-eight subjects were distributed across four experimental conditions, using the pollution paradigm. As before, half the subjects received a flexible text, and half received a rigid one. A further experimental manipulation was introduced just before the subjects began to read the texts.

In a "psychologization" condition, the experimenter informed the subjects that, after they had read the text, they would be asked to guess the main personality characteristics of the author: "We are interested in finding out how far people are able to judge correctly a person's personality on the basis of something he or she has written . . ."

In another condition ("content"), subjects were focused on the content of the text: "We are interested in finding out how far people are able to give a summary of the essential points of a text after reading it just once . . ."

After reading the text, the subjects filled in the opinion questionnaire once more, then the source image questionnaire. Finally, all subjects wrote a summary of the text.

Results

There were no significant effects at the level of the image of the minority, although there was a tendency for subjects to judge the source more positively when they had been focused on the content of the message rather than the personality of the source. The effects of flexibility/rigidity on the image were virtually nil. What degree of influence occurred, then, in the various conditions? The influence scores are given in Table 19.

TABLE 19
Mean opinion changes ($n = 22$)

	Direct	Indirect
Flexible minority, "psychologization"	+0·01	+0·85
Rigid minority, "psychologization"	+0·06	+0·94
Flexible minority, "content"	+0·76	+1·09
Rigid minority, "content"	+0·60	+0·61

Taking the results in their order of interest, first, the effect of "psychologization" operated somewhat indistinctly, regardless of whether the source was rigid or flexible ($F = 4\cdot811$, $d.f.$ 1/84; $P < \cdot05$). Compared to previous experiments, two things appear to have happened. First, psychologization has had no effect on the influence of the rigid source, and it is as if rigidity brings about psychologization of its own accord. Thus, it is the influence of the flexible source which is mainly affected by psychologization: direct influence is blocked, and displaced onto the *indirect* items. Essentially, psychologization appears to block the acceptance of minority positions which have been explicitly stated.

The effect of focusing the population on content, in contrast, is very largely positive, whether on *indirect* or *direct* items ($F = 0\cdot850$, $d.f.$ 1/84; not significant). The effect on the *direct* items is, nevertheless, the most striking: in all of our studies there have been very few conditions which have shown subjects openly approaching minority positions. If this has happened, it has been mostly when a flexible minority source was not explicitly identified as a minority. Furthermore, it is remarkable that focusing on the content of the minority message allows even a rigid source to have this much influence. Why should this be the case? It is for reasons which we have already seen but which this time have become more explicit: to focus on the content means that any image of the source is not made use of, and thus the source evades categorization, whether in terms of rigid personality or of minority status. *There-

fore it becomes clear that it is through the act of categorization itself that the population comes to reject minority influence.

Even so, negotiation does have a role in conditions where subjects are focused on content: when the content is rigid, it tends to have slightly less influence ($F = 3{\cdot}118$, *d.f.* 1/84; $P < {\cdot}10$), although this is only true for the *indirect* items ($F = 3{\cdot}446$, *d.f.* 1/84; $P < {\cdot}10$). However, unlike in previous experiments, this is a matter of degree: the minority position has still "penetrated"—and this is the essential point—to the *direct* items—items on which we have usually found either no effect at all or sometimes even a negative effect.

Finally, it should be noted that these results are remarkably consistent with those of Experiment 6, which at first sight seemed to be contradictory. Since we had expected, in line with previous results, to find as much influence on *direct* as on *indirect* items with a flexible text, the absence of influence on *direct* items even with a flexible minority was surprising. This result is understandable in the light of the present experiment, however: it is explained by the experimental manipulation itself, which very directly induced subjects to interpret minority positions in psychological terms.

The next experiment provides further confirmation of this effect of psychologization.

Experiment 9: Rigidity and psychologization: a confirmation (Mugny and Papastamou, 1980)

The subjects were 24 second-year psychology students taking part in introductory seminars on methods in experimental social psychology. There were two experimental conditions, with 12 students in each. All the students were Swiss, and sex was controlled for in the allocation to conditions.

(a) Attitude scaling

The questionnaire already described for Experiment 1 was used to assess attitudes toward the Swiss national army. This questionnaire provided 40 adjectives with which the subjects expressed their agreement or disagreement as applied to the army, encircling a "yes" or a "no" which flanked each adjective. Beforehand, these adjectives had been judged by about 40 subjects who had classified them as being either favourable or unfavourable towards the army. In the present experiment we used two parallel forms of the questionnaire, each comprising 20 adjectives and being responded to either on pre-test or post-test.

Half of the adjectives were positive, and half were negative, making it possible to calculate an evaluative index of the positiveness of attitudes toward the army. This score was obtained by subtracting the number of negative items accepted from the number of positive items accepted. A score of $+10$ indicates a resolutely positive attitude; a score of -10 indicates an extremely negative attitude. Because of the disparity between the two parallel forms of the questionnaire, we transformed each individual's score into a z score for both the pre-test and the post-test, and these z scores were used in the analysis of variance.

(b) Procedure

The experiment was presented to the subjects as being a part of their course in experimental methods; specifically, as a demonstration of the measurement of social judgements. First, the subjects filled in one page of the questionnaire on which they were to give their attitude towards the Swiss army on an 8-point scale ranging from "absolutely in favour" to "absolutely against". This was intended to introduce the army as the theme of the experiment; in fact all the subjects opted for negative evaluations of the army. Next, the subjects filled in the first form of the questionnaire described above. During the second phase of the experiment, each subject individually read a tract. No other communication was permitted.

Next, the subjects described the presumed authors of the text by selecting from a list of adjectives, which varied as a manipulation of the independent variable. Finally, subjects filled in the second version of the army attitude questionnaire. The session terminated with a discussion about the aims of the experiment and the methods used.

The text, which was the rigid version of the text already used in Experiment 1 was a one-page tract defending an extreme left-wing anti-militarist position and calling for struggle "within and against the army, so that the dictatorship of the proletariat may triumph". The text was written in the "traditional" style of extreme left-wing groups.

(c) Political and psycho-political description of the source

After having read the tract and before responding to the second form of the attitude questionnaire, the subjects were asked to describe the presumed authors of the tract, on the basis of their reading in this session alone. They were given one of two lists of adjectives, according to the experimental condition.

In the "political" condition, the subjects were to describe the authors in purely political terms, choosing one or more adjectives from a list of 12: anarchist, apolitical, conservative, fascist, left-wing, liberal, marxist, nationalist, progressive, reactionary, reformist, and revolutionary.

In the "psycho-political" condition, 12 adjectives referring to psychological traits were mixed in with the above list. These had been obtained from our questionnaire assessing the minority image: arrogant, understanding, confused, efficient, intolerant, irresponsible, open, diffident, resolute, rigid, demanding, straightforward.

(d) Results

Here we are concerned only with the responses to the attitude questionnaire. The number of adjectives used relating to the image of the source was in fact very reduced compared to the original questionnaire which we normally used for this assessment, because in this case we used the adjectives only to induce perceptions of the source, either in political or in psycho-political terms only.

For the statistical analysis, it will be recalled that we used transformed (z) scores because of the parallelism between the two forms of the attitude questionnaire. However, in Table 20 we give the raw-score means, which are easier to read.

TABLE 20

Evaluative scores relating to the army, before and after reading the tract $(n = 6)$

	Before	After
Extreme subjects/psycho-political	−8·67	−8·67
Extreme subjects/political	−8·50	−9·00
Moderate subjects/psycho-political	−5·00	−5·33
Moderate subjects/political	−4·83	−7·67

We have separated subjects whose negative attitude towards the army was "moderate" (raw scores up to -7) from those whose attitude was "extreme" (-8 and -9), since for the latter subjects a ceiling effect could prevent any influence from becoming apparent.

The results appear to confirm our hypothesis that perception of the source solely in political terms would lead to greater influence than a perception which included both political and psychological dimensions. Let us examine the effect more closely.

First, as we had foreseen, there was a large ceiling effect in that half of the subjects had little room for change because of their initial extremism. The moderate/extreme factor was very highly significant ($F = 23·244$, $d.f.$ $1/20$; $P < ·0005$). We considered influence separately for these two groups of subjects, concentrating on the moderates. Thus, although the interaction of the experimental variable with the pre-test/post-test dependent variable is only slight for the population considered as a whole ($F = 3·982$, $d.f.$ $1/20$; $P < ·07$), if we look at the moderate subjects alone, we find that the interaction is significant for them: $F = 5·407$, $d.f.$ $1/20$; $P < ·05$. In the case of those moderate subjects whose induced image of the minority included mixed political and psychological dimensions, there was no significant difference between the pre-test and the post-test scores, indicating that no influence took place. In contrast, an attitude change did occur in those moderate subjects whose induced image was purely political. This polarization, which occurred in spite of the singleness of the source and its rigidity, suggests that we were indeed successful in engaging a mechanism of minority influence: psychologization, a specific variety of naturalization, constitutes an obstacle, an ideological one, to minority influence. This is demonstrated by the fact that if this process is counteracted by inducing a "non-naturalizing" image of the source, influence is released.

Conclusions

Chapter 4 showed the effects of rigidity: it diminishes influence, essentially on items directly linked with the minority position. Chapter 5 confirmed these effects and localized them in specific inter-individual contexts. This chapter attempted to reveal the mechanism through which rigidity has its effects.

Our account of this mechanism was already beginning to take shape from the first chapters, since we early introduced assessment of the minority image into the experimental paradigms. Sometimes the results were clear, as in Experiment 2, where we obtained a positive correlation between the degree of perceived consistency and flexibility. But we did not find such results systematically repeated in the following experiments, no doubt because there is bound to be some interference between the opinion ratings used to measure opinion change and the image assessment which was always carried out after the opinion rating. It became obvious that a direct experimental approach would have to be taken to the question of the effect of the minority image: variables relating to the image itself would have to be manipulated, especially since we were seeking the psychosociological mechanism of influence at the level of perception of the minority. This approach has now been attempted, and we are in a position to better understand the multiple and complex articulations involved in the population's representation of the minority.

First, it appears that the induction alone of a flexible or rigid image can lead to different effects for the same minority position, therefore to characterize any given minority position merely as flexible or rigid is insufficient: no position is, in itself, flexible or rigid. Even if some positions are inherently more likely to be perceived as rigid than others, it is still the perception of them as such which is essential.

Once the rigidity of a minority has been "recognized" by a population, a more pronounced structuring of the image takes place: the dimension relating to blocking behaviour is given central position and seems to colour all other judgements, even as far as the evaluation of consistency, which, as we already know, is necessary for the diffusion of minority innovations. However, this effect is not automatic: for it to appear, subjects must already be judging the minority with only a limited number of dimensions. This is shown by Ricateau's experiment, which diminished the influence of a consistent minority by reducing the number of rating scales on which subjects were able to give their evaluations of the minority.

But even this is not the complete picture: even after it has been "recognized", rigidity does not necessarily determine the way in which new opinions are established. For this, the rigidity itself has to be interpreted as being the source and explanation of minority behaviours. Rigidity may, in turn, be perceived as the result of certain predispositions or personality traits of the minority (or even of psychosocial characteristics, such as *esprit de corps*, or in-group mentality). It may also be seen as the inevitable consequence of a given social situation or as the simple, coherent, symbolic reflex of a social state of affairs which the minority is merely ushering to its logical conclusion.

We went on to consider naturalization as an essential ideological mechanism mediating the relations between dominant and dominated groups. Naturalization appears to be a process which confers a certain "functional" role on rigidity: it allows the behaviours of a minority to be individualized and thus removed from the context of social relations which in reality determine them. More specifically, psychologization allows minority behaviours to be perceived and explained in terms of psychological characteristics of the source (we have pointed out other possible forms of naturalization in Chapter 3). Thus, we saw that individualization of the source facilitates the appearance of the usual effects of rigidity, while the existence of more than one source prevents individualization from taking place. By the same token, the induction in the population of a "psychologized" image of the minority facilitates the effects of rigidity, even when the minority is relatively flexible, whereas focusing the population on the content of the minority message (thus distracting attention from inherent characteristics of the source) releases the power of the minority to influence.

Ideological mechanisms, then, appear to be smoothly articulated with intrasituational variations: experimental situations may facilitate or inhibit these mechanisms, because subjects share certain normative and ideological orientations. Experimentation, therefore, does not obscure or leave out of account the social insertion of our subjects; on the contrary, this is mobilized and brought into explicit and salient operation by the type of experiments we have carried out. What processes bring this about? In the final chapter, we shall try to show that this takes place through a redefinition of social identity within certain normative contexts which we shall describe.

7

Minority influence and psychosocial identity

We have now almost completed the experimental approach to our object of study. In the preceding chapters, we have shown the effects of different styles of flexible and rigid behaviours. We have studied the variations of these effects in different social situations. We have also shown the vital explanatory value of the modes of perception of the minority by the population in understanding how the population allows the minority to exert influence. But does the population allow the minority to influence, or does it in fact allow itself to be influenced?

The preceding chapter, as well as illustrating the role of representations in minority influence, also led us to see the intervention of ideological mechanisms as a necessary component in the "spontaneous" judgements of our subjects. One of these mechanisms, a very important one, is rooted in the antagonistic relationship between power and minority. Power disseminates an ideological interpretation of antagonistic minority behaviours: naturalization. Several experiments have shown how such naturalization, when incorporated into an experimental situation in the form of psychologization, diminishes the power of even a flexible minority to influence. On the other hand, we have seen how certain conditions can dissipate the usual effects of rigidity: specifically, conditions under which the possibility of a naturalizing attribution is removed or at least reduced, namely when several independent minorities prevent individualization, when the situation is seen solely in political terms, and when attention is focused on the content of the minority message. All of these conditions prevent the activation of the ideological mechanisms which normally come into play when the minority identity of the source is made explicit.

..e intervention of a special mode of attribution (naturalization and its consequences on minority influence) when the population is confronted with a minority implies at the very least that the minority character of the source has been perceived. We arrive, then, at the following hypothesis: *a flexible minority, by means of its very flexibility, masks the deviancy of its social identity; the rigidity of the rigid minority makes its deviancy explicit.*

This hypothesis follows naturally from our results:

Rigidity tends to create more resistance to influence than does flexibility;

Merely identifying a source as a minority is sufficient to bring about the effects typical of rigidity, even when the source is flexible;

Focusing on the identity of the minority source also brings about resistance, while "distraction" from this identity appears to remove barriers to minority influence.

We have shown that rigidity, as we have operationalized it, makes the minority identity of the source salient within the antagonistic relationship; the question naturally follows as to the role of the experimental subjects' own psychosocial identity. In their approach to or avoidance of minority responses, the subjects equally imply something as to their identification or non-identification with the source's social group or category.

In two experiments, we shall show that this question of the subjects' psychosocial identity can be answered in terms of normative contexts. A third experiment pursues this same approach by setting up situations in which the minority message is presented as being explicitly concerned with membership in the minority group, thus making approach or avoidance of minority positions determinants in the redefinition of social identity. The final experiment will show that the obstacles peculiar to the rigid minority can be lifted, to the extent that subjects can be brought to share categorial affiliations with the minority.

Experiment 10: Rigidity and minority identity

Experiment 10 will not be described here in its entirety—only those details essential for the particular demonstration will be reported. The pollution paradigm was used, but with the rather large difference that the opinion questionnaire was filled in only once, at the end of the experiment. The subjects read the usual text (without the slogans) and then judged it on a 100-point scale, measuring one of two dimensions according to the experimental condition:

In the first condition, the subjects were asked to judge how far the text was politically majority- or minority-related. The scale was made meaningful in this context by suggesting to the subjects that they could indicate on it the percentage of government members they thought would agree with a particular opinion. In this condition, then, we focused the subjects on a political dimension, in a way rendering explicit the antagonistic relationships which might underlie the experimental situation.

In the second condition, the subjects judged how far the text was numerically majority- or minority-related. To make the scale meaningful in this condition, we compared it to an opinion poll, which would give the percentage of the population holding a particular opinion. As opinion polls also tend to do, this condition obscured the issue of power relations. The minority character of the text would therefore have been less explicit in the second condition.

After judging the text, the subjects received both the flexible and the rigid slogans which had previously been removed from the texts (the order of presentation being controlled). These slogans were in turn judged according to their minority or majority character, that is, in numerical or political terms, according to the experimental condition. The subjects then gave their opinion on the usual 100-point scale.

Results

Table 21 gives the mean scores in each condition for the text, and for the flexible and rigid slogans separately.

Considering the text alone, it is clear that its minority character was not perceived, or at least the position it represents was not perceived as being particularly incompatible with the dominant position. In fact, when the first experiments were carried out, the text appeared as clearly minority, but the position it represents later came to be more

accepted. The effects of our induction of numerical or political judgements are therefore especially important, because the text tends to
appear more minority-related in political terms than in numerical
terms ($F = 3.352$, d.f. 1/43, $P < .10$). We can, in fact, conclude from
this that our subjects were under no illusions about the nature of the
text; it was enough to place it within the context of an antagonistic
relationship (simply by asking subjects to judge it in political terms)
for its non-majority character to become apparent.

TABLE 21
Mean judgements of minority (0) or majority (100) character

		Slogans	
	Text	Flexible	Rigid
In numerical terms ($n = 24$)	61·25	57·08	39·16
In political terms ($n = 21$)	49·52	63·81	29·52

Rigid slogans would appear to be peculiarly apt to make the minority character of their source salient, because they appear to be judged
as very obviously minority-related, significantly more so than the flexible slogans ($F = 55.159$, d.f. 1/43, $P < .0005$), which appear themselves as slightly "majority". The rigid tracts, then, spontaneously
activated the ideological mechanisms relating to minorities which we
have studied in the preceding chapters. The ambiguous character of
the flexible texts also explains how merely identifying the source as a
minority is accepted as plausible by the subjects and can induce similar mechanisms.

The difference between judgements of the flexible and rigid slogans
is significant in both experimental conditions. It will be noticed, however, that this difference is sharply increased when political judgements are induced, compared with numerical judgements (interaction: $F = 5.633$, d.f. 1/43, $P < .025$). This is congruent with the tendency of judgements relative to the text itself, whose minority character was somewhat more apparent when political judgements were
induced.

Did the type of judgement induced play any role in the establishment of opinions? We can determine this by comparing the responses

to the opinion questionnaire in the two conditions. Table 22 gives the comparison (it will be recalled that the rating used in this experiment was, exceptionally, an 11-point one: 0 = agreement, 10 = disagreement).

The analysis of variance showed a significant interaction between the two factors ($F = 4.056$, $d.f.$ 1/43, $P < .05$), indicating that there was no difference on the *indirect* items ($F = 0.243$, $d.f.$ 1/43) but that there was a significant difference on the *direct* items between the two conditions ($F = 5.547$, $d.f.$ 1/43, $P < .025$). It was in fact the subjects who had been induced to respond in political terms whose opinions were closest to the minority position.

In this particular experiment, of course, we have to *assume* that an influence process has taken place, since we do not have a pre-test opinion rating. However, the results are consistent with those obtained previously. Thus, Experiment 8 on the effects of psychologization brought about a sharp reduction of influence on *direct* items, while focusing on content allowed similar degrees of influence on both *direct* and *indirect* items. Furthermore, whatever type of induction we carried out (i.e. psychologization or "content"), the same degree of influence appeared on the *indirect* items. The two sets of results are therefore identical. But does not judgement in numerical terms lead to the notion of rarity, which is one of the aspects of the psychologization process we have looked at, while judgement in political terms perhaps could be seen as dealing with the question on its own, "proper" ground, thus removing the barrier to minority influence which naturalization, in contrast, raises?

TABLE 22
Mean opinion ratings

	Direct	Indirect
Numerical judgements	4·52	6·40
Political judgements	3·63	6·58

It will be recalled also that in Experiment 8 there was strong influence on the *direct* items in the "content" condition, despite the fact that the minority identity of the source was explicit. The fact that these similar results were obtained in very different situations suggests more than just a fortunate coincidence.

At this point, we need to make explicit a further basic articulation. We now know that rigidity encounters barriers to its influence because it carries with it some sort of signal identifying it as a minority. We also know that these barriers are erected only because the minority has been categorized in a particular way, which in turn is the result of ideological processes which appear to be activated automatically when the minority identity of a source becomes apparent. Yet we have also seen that this sequence of events is not inevitable; in particular, it may be avoided when situational factors are unfavourable to such an act of categorization; in this case, the rigid minority essentially increases its influence on the most socially overt responses.

How can we include such apparently diverse effects within the same theoretical framework? The relevant articulation will be sought at the level of social identity. Some such phenomenon as social identity is, moreover, clearly implied in social influence situations. To approach a minority is, in effect, to identify oneself (*vis-à-vis* oneself and/or society) to some extent with the minority. In such situations, the activation of a normative context must be an essential factor. If negative connotations already cling to the minority position, identification with it must be difficult. Furthermore, such connotations emphasize the socially deviant character of the minority, and this will facilitate the activation of ideological blocking mechanisms (which will, in turn, further encourage the perception of negative connotations associated with minority positions).

Conversely, if a normative context of a different kind is brought about, namely one in which "minority" has positive connotations, such as in terms of social originality, then identification of a particular minority in such terms will be facilitated and by the same token the activation of ideological mechanisms which would lead to the stigmatization of the minority will be inhibited.

Normative context and psychosocial identity

The results of the last experiment are crucial for our thesis. We already knew, of course, that rigidity in minority behaviours is not a phenomenon "in itself", but rather a result at the representational level of complex articulations among factors at different levels. What the last experiment added to this was that rigidity at the representational level corresponds to an interpretation which flows from the explicit identification of the source as a minority. This result validates our operational definition of the flexibility/rigidity variable. In our series of experiments, we defined this variable early on in terms of the ideological nature of the compromises conceded by the minority. Having started out with an ideological interpretation, we now return to it after having made explicit the complex articulation which occurs at the level of the population's perceptions of the minority.

This experiment also brought to light an additional aspect: even when the minority character of a stance has been recognized, it can still exert influence, on condition that the population is focused on its political dimension. Why should this be so?

Once it has been perceived, the minority identity of a source must be placed within a normative context, which itself is able to vary. We can certainly suppose that its deviant character (if it is the type of deviance which has negative connotations) will assume salience almost automatically, because for this to occur is an ideological mechanism current in our social system. In certain situations, however, it is possible for different norms to be activated, such as one relating to originality. In this case, what would take place would be a positive evaluation of opinions which would be perceived as progressive, and oriented toward constructive social change.

Such connotations must be important for what we have called social identity. Let us look at this notion, based on recent work by the Bristol school (Tajfel, 1978; Turner, 1978), in more detail. Social identification can be understood as the sum of social categorizations which are considered by the individual to be part of their self-definition. In other words, social identity is the set of an individual's social identifications. Such a definition of social identity, although summary, has the advantage of including within it the aspect of group relations. By "identification" we understand certain broad and relatively permanent categorizations, but also some more contingent ones, more the result of specific social situations. An essential feature of this conception is the individual's search for a positive identity, which is often acquired precisely through identification with a social category or a social group which is judged in positive terms.

We can, therefore, consider social influence situations, and particularly those in which minority influence attempts take place, as situations which involve the redefinition of social identity. In effect, the positions put forward in such situations refer back to social groups or social categories, whose identity plays a crucial role in the outcome: thus, for example, the situations we have set up experimentally create relations between "majority" and minority groups. Whether they are influenced or not, positively or negatively, individuals will redefine their social identity in terms of the social group or category which they approach or distance themselves from. To approach toward a minority is to redefine oneself as a member, or at least as a sympathizer, with the minority group. To distance oneself from it is to re-affirm one's majority identity, or even to deny any possibility of a minority identity, *to identify oneself with a minority is to attribute to oneself the characteristics stereotypically associated with the minority.*

Such an identification poses many problems for the individual. In some normative contexts (those which make the minority's deviant character salient), we have seen how ideological mechanisms operate to naturalize minority behaviours. This is a contemporary ideological treatment of deviance. It is also possible to state, although we have not treated this experimentally here, that deviance also gives rise to forms of treatment which are repressive. It is therefore easily imagined that, in situations where these ideological mechanisms are activated, social identification with the minority has certain hazards; in fact, to identify oneself with a minority is to run the same risks that the minority runs, since this identification involves attributing to oneself the characteristics of the minority. Thus, one risks being naturalized oneself, even repressed. In such cases, we can with reason speak (with Larsen, 1974) of the social costs of identification.

If, then, minority effects are characterized by difficulty in modifying socially explicit responses, it is because the dominant mode of treatment of minority behaviours tends to make explicit the negative connotations which attach to minority identity.

On the other hand, obviously it is not always the dominant normative context which is activated in social situations, otherwise social evolution could never take place. Thus, there are certain conditions in which it is possible to evaluate minority behaviours in terms of the potentiality they represent for bringing about social change, or at least contributing actively to it. Moscovici and Lage (1978) have shown how, in a situation involving perceptual judgements, the activation of originality norms (as opposed to the accuracy norms which are usually dominant in such a situation) led to a considerable increase in the influence of the minority.

The next two experiments attempt to induce, within a social judgement situation, not only norms relating to deviance (thus imputing negative connotations to minority behaviours) but also norms relating to social originality (thus imputing positive connotations). In the latter case, it can easily be imagined that influence should increase, if it is true that influence works through the redefinition of social identity.

A similar norm has already been activated in several of our experiments (though indirectly), by focusing subjects on the content of the minority message and by setting up more than one independent, but similar, minority sources. It is also possible—and this is the aim of the next experiments—to make this norm explicit, in particular by causing subjects to believe that we were assessing their capacity for social independence or originality.

Conceptualizing social influence as redefinition of social identity causes our different results to fall into a more integrated pattern. First of all, it becomes clear why influence is often less on *direct* items, because these not only reproduce minority positions verbatim, they are also the items which, if the subjects accepted them, would bring them closest to the source. It is therefore not surprising that it is on these items above all that subjects refuse to yield when the minority character of the positions put forward is made explicit for one reason or another: these items are the most closely identified with the minority character itself.

It also becomes understandable that influence can be equal on both types of item when the source is flexible, because, as we have seen, in this case the minority character of the source is obscured and ideological mechanisms which would act to stigmatize deviance are not brought into play. Identification is thus easier. It also becomes clear why even a flexible text can have the same effects as a rigid one, when the minority identity of the source is made explicit.

Converse effects are explained by the same reasons: the obstacles to minority influence are removed when subjects are focused on what we have called a norm of social change, as in the situations in which we focused subjects on the politics or the content of the minority message; in such cases, the question of negative identity is side-stepped.

The concept of social identity interacting with various normative contexts has considerable explanatory power, since it gives pattern to a set of widely varying effects. For the moment, however, this explanatory organization of our data is only *a posteriori*. Proposing it now as a hypothesis, we proceed to the final four experiments.

Initially, we consider two of them. The first experiment does not include an influence manipulation: instead, we simply show that the expression of extreme or radical opinions is facilitated when a norm of originality is explicit in the context but inhibited when the context focuses on the negative connotations of deviance. The second experiment sets up two similar contexts but reintroduces the test/retest paradigm which permits assessment of the impact of a minority source.

Experiment 11: Polarization of judgements and normative contexts

The assimilation/contrast theory predicts that individuals holding an extreme position will give a more extreme judgement regarding propositions relating to their attitude object. This assumption has in fact formed the basis of certain attitude scales, such as Thurstone's. However, Zavalloni and Cook (1965), and later Eiser and Stroebe (1972) have shown that the assumption is correct only when there is congruence between individuals' opinions and the positive evaluative connotations of the judgement scale itself.

If we take an example from our national army paradigm, suppose that an anti-militarist is asked to judge propositions in terms of pacifism/violence. It will be easy to give an extreme response: to judge the propositions one rejects as extremely violent is at the same time to make a negative judgement on them; by the same token, to judge one's own anti-militarist position as pacifist is at the same time to enhance one's self-image. But suppose that the same individual has to judge the same propositions, but on the basis of loyalty to one's country.

The tendency will be to make less extreme responses, because one's own position takes on less positive connotations in this context, while the opposed militarist position takes on more positive connotations.

In more recent work, Eiser and his colleagues (Eiser and Ross, 1977; Eiser and Pancer, 1979) have examined this effect further by using pro-attitudinal advocates (contrary to the cognitive dissonance studies), who were asked in pleading their case either to use positively tinged words for their own position and negatively tinged ones for the opposed case, or to use positively tinged words for the opposed case and negatively tinged ones for their own. In the latter case, judgements about one's own position were moderated; it must surely be difficult to give open expression to an opinion which has been given a negative (or less positive) connotation. It seems likely that the notion of psychosocial identity is also relevant to studies of this type.

We used a similar paradigm in the present experiment, although we did not use the notion of connotation as conferring a single value, either positive or negative, on a particular behaviour. A normative context which is negative toward deviance or positive toward original-ity is more than the activation of a set of evaluative connotations. What is activated is a set of social representations and ideological mechanisms whose nature we have already seen (naturalization, threat of repression, etc.).

At this point, we aim to evaluate the predictive power of concep-tualizing the processes we have been studying in terms of psychosocial identity. One prediction of this hypothesis is that the distance between source and receiver must have an important effect. It is the subjects closest to the minority position who are most exposed to the pos-sibilities of identification with the minority, and so they should be most sensitive to the normative context. In contrast, moderate sub-jects should be less aware of this risk, since by virtue of holding a mod-erate position alone, they are sufficiently distant from the minority posi-tion to run no risk of being assimilated to it.

We would like to include a short digression here: it has often been stated that influence increases with distance (up to an optimal dis-tance). This function has been interpreted in terms of a "ceiling" effect (the most extreme subjects being least able to shift their position) or in terms of increasing pressure. Would it not be better to reconsider all such effects in terms of social identification? This would restore the social dimension to studies which appear to have stripped the social influence process of precisely its social significance.

THE EXPERIMENT

The subjects were 46 students from our introductory course in social psychology. At the beginning of a class, the instructor asked for their help for a short time in perfecting a questionnaire about attitudes toward the national army. Unanimous agreement was obtained, and the experimenter asked half the subjects to leave the room (the subjects were seated side by side around arranged tables, and each alternate person was asked to leave the room). The session lasted less than ten minutes, then the first subjects left, and the second half of the class came back into the room to be subjects in turn. There was no verbal communication between the two sets of subjects. The "originality" condition was implemented first. At the end of the experiment, part of the class participated in a discussion about the hypotheses, and the students' reaction to the session.

(a) The questionnaire

There were seven questions, and the response was to select a number between 0 and 100 on a scale. To the first question, the response was to indicate how far one was for (0) or against (100) the national army. For the remaining six questions, the same scale was used, but going from "politically extreme right" (0) to "politically extreme left" (100).

The response to the second question was to indicate one's own position on the scale, i.e. whether left or right, and how far.

The next five items were to judge the following five propositions, which were presented orally by the experimenter:

3. "The national army constitutes a terrible danger to our liberties." (A very vague left-wing item, expressing no specific left-wing ideology. Not surprisingly, the item was not discriminating, so we did not include it in our analysis.)
4. "The national army is the essential guarantee of our liberties." (Right-wing item, traditional militarist position.)
5. "The national army is a social weapon against the workers." ("Traditional" left-wing item.)

6. "Yes to national defence, no to an army of repression." (*Moderate* item.)
7. "The army is a repressive state apparatus opposed to the dictatorship of the proletariat." (Left-wing item with extreme left-wing phraseology.)

Each question was presented orally, and repeated, before subjects wrote down their responses. They were asked not to revise any of their responses.

(b) Experimental manipulations

Experimental manipulations consisted in presenting the questionnaire either as an assessment of social originality or as an assessment of deviance. This was done by telling the subjects that the experimenter was interested not so much in attitudes toward the army as in measuring tendencies toward originality or deviance.

In the originality condition, the experimenter said: "This is not so much a measure of opinions as a measure of tendencies toward social originality, a sort of measure of independence".

In the deviance condition, he said: "This is not so much a measure of opinions, as a measure of tendencies toward social deviance; this is important at a time when there is increasing repression, especially against conscientious objectors".

During an explanation of how the measures had been arrived at, the experimenter discreetly referred several more times to the ostensible interest of the research: social originality or social deviance.

(c) Extreme subjects and moderate subjects

As expected, all subjects were opposed to the army. On the first question (0 = for the army, 100 = against) the mean score was close to 80. When, as in the second question, the judgement was to be made about oneself, the scores were less extreme: the mean was around 64 (a score of 100 representing "extreme left"). We can suppose that this second measure is a better discriminator, because the following items also call for political judgements, while the first item could be responded to in other than political terms, such as religious reasons. We therefore decided to divide the population into two groups on the basis of their responses to the second question. We expected a difference in the effect of the originality/deviance variable according to whether the subjects were more or less left-wing, and we expected the effect to be greatest in the case of the more left-wing subjects, since social identification with deviance or originality is more likely in their case.

We considered as extreme those subjects who gave a response to the second question of at least 65 (of whom there were 9 in the originality condition and 14 in the deviance condition). The mean for these subjects was around 75, which indicates a clearly left-wing position. We categorized as moderate those subjects giving responses up to 60 (of whom there were 12 in the originality condition and 11 in the deviance condition). The mean for these subjects was around 52, thus justifying their designation as "moderate".

(d) Results

The results given in Table 23 show the mean judgement scores for the right-wing item, the moderate item, and for the two left-wing items ("traditional" and "extreme"). We carried out a two-way analysis of variance on each item, except for the right-wing item, for which the distributions between experimental conditions were too dissimilar. In this case, we compared the two experimental conditions using a non-parametric test.

These results are particularly clear-cut. There are few differences between the originality and deviance conditions for the moderate subjects, just as we would expect, given that the negative/positive norms induced do not apply to these subjects themselves. For the extreme subjects, in contrast, the picture is very different. They would have been more personally affected by these connotations because they had revealed themselves as being definitely "left-wing". Accordingly, the experimental manipulation did affect their responses. On the one hand, the right-wing item is judged as more right-wing by subjects in the originality condition than by subjects in the deviance condition (who had been reminded of the social costs of deviance): Mann-Whitney's $U = 24 \cdot 5$, $d.f.$ 14/9; one-tailed $P < \cdot 01$. On the other hand, the left-wing items are judged more to the left by subjects in the originality condition (traditional left-wing item: $F = 4 \cdot 805$, $d.f.$ 1/42, $P < \cdot 05$; extreme left-wing item: $F = 7 \cdot 189$, $d.f.$ 1/42, $P < \cdot 025$). At this point it is interesting to note that, in the deviance condition, there is practically no difference between the moderate item (which is moderate but in fact also pro-militarist), and the traditional left-wing item. Despite the reductionism of the experimental situation, it is as if something like a centre–left coalition has been created! In the originality condition, in contrast, variety within the extreme left is clearly seen, as though splinter groups were emerging.

These results call for several comments. The first is the clear importance of distinguishing between moderate and extreme subjects. To introduce such a distinction is not to fall into the error of "psychologizing" but rather to take account of the fact that it is the subjects who express the most radical positions who are most able to perceive the possibility of identification with a minority position. It is

TABLE 23
Mean judgement scores

	Right	Moderate	Traditional left	Extreme left
MODERATE SUBJECTS				
Originality	24·58	55·42	82·92	78·33
Deviance	11·36	48·18	82·73	88·18
EXTREME SUBJECTS				
Originality	3·67	55·56	79·33	94·89
Deviance	18·71	50·71	56·71	70·00

therefore not surprising that, if the minority position has negative connotations conferred upon it (such as social deviance), it is these extreme subjects who will be most inhibited in the expression of extreme judgements. While judging themselves as left-wing, these subjects also seem to have "de-dramatized" their own positions, since they judged even the moderate item as being almost as left-wing as the traditional left-wing item. We shall return to this point in the following experiments.

The second comment is that we finally appear to have managed to bring about some sort of influence, without having specified any particular minority position: the effects seen here are similar to those we have usually seen in connection with a minority source. This is not to say that minority influence can be reduced to a simple effect of evaluative connotations. The effect of such connotations, although clearly essential, are only one link in a long chain of articulations which culminate in minority phenomena. What we have here is one example of the consequences of power's implicit discourse on norms: when, by means of the experimental situation, subjects are reminded of the "social costs" of deviance, the expression of progressive positions becomes less possible.

But do such norms, in fact, have any impact on minority influence?

Experiment 12: Normative context and minority influence (Mugny *et al.*, 1981)

This experiment aims to replicate the effects found in the preceding experiment at the level of minority influence and within the pollution paradigm.

Almost 150 subjects took part in the experiment, which was completed in a single session. The subjects responded to the usual questionnaire, read a minority text, and then responded to the opinion questionnaire once more. The large number of subjects enabled the inclusion of the variable of distance between subjects and minority positions. After some subjects had been randomly discarded, to equalize the numbers in conditions, 144 subjects remained, with 36 in each experimental condition. Within each condition, 18 subjects were relatively close to the source, and 18 relatively distant.

The experimental design, then, included 3 variables:

The normative context, in terms of deviance or originality;

The minority position was either flexible or rigid;

The subjects were either close to or distant from the minority position; we expected that those subjects close to the minority would be most reticent in expressing their agreement with it.

The operationalization of the deviance/originality and proximity/distance of the subjects from the minority are new and will be described in detail.

(a) Induction of normative context (originality or deviance)

Just before the subjects read the text, the normative context was induced by means of a passage written on the front cover of the text and the experimenter's reading-out of the instructions. Eight classes took part in the experiment, four being assigned to the deviance context and four to the originality context. The rigid and flexible versions of the text were distributed at random within each class.

The exact instructions for the originality condition were as follows (the deviance version is indicated in brackets):

> Now we are going to ask you to read a text on the problem of pollution. This text was produced by an ecology group which is, in political terms, a minority fringe group. In this second part of the experiment we want to find measures which will enable us to detect, as objectively as possible, individual tendencies towards *originality* (*deviance*) in people who read the text. So we ask you to read the text we are going to give out very carefully and to answer the three questions which come after the text.

These three questions were: "How far do you judge this text to be *original* (*deviant*)?"; "How far do you agree or disagree with the text?"; and "How far do you judge yourself to have tendencies toward *originality* (*deviance*)?". Subjects responded to these questions on a 12-point scale.

Originality and deviance were defined thus: "*Originality* (*deviance*) can be defined as the tendency to accept new values and ideas which are *moving in the direction of social progress* (*socially rejected because they call established norms into question*)".

Two of the three questions which followed the text also served to remind subjects of the reference norm we were attempting to induce, and thus to reinforce it.

(b) Proximity and distance of subjects from the minority position

The technique used to distinguish between subjects was similar to that used in the preceding experiment and consisted in examining the distribution obtained from the total number of subjects and "cutting" the curve at its mid-point. The numbers thus assigned to each condition ("close" and "distant") were equalized by discarding a number of subjects at random. Such a technique is not without disadvantages, but it serves as a preliminary means of investigation. More sophisticated analyses would no doubt have been more powerful, but if we were to find differences, even with such a simple technique, our hypothesis would receive strong support.

What criterion was used to set up the distribution? The *direct* items were most sensitive to recognition of the minority status of the source, but responses to the *indirect* items were not without relevance. We decided to base our division of subjects into two categories on both types of item. This decision was supported by several reasons. The analysis of results would be based on both types of measure, and to have differentiated subjects according to only one of them would obviously have been to introduce a bias. But more important was the fact that each subject would be making use of a sort of "personal equation" which would lead the individual, for instance, to be either more, or less, in agreement with the whole set of items. It is clear, then, that for example a mean of 3 on the *direct* items would have a different meaning according to whether the mean for the *indirect* items was 2 or 4, let us say. In the first case, the subject prefers the *indirect* items to the *direct*, and is thus more opposed to the minority position. In the second case, the subject is clearly closer, overall, to the minority position.

We therefore based our division of subjects into *close* and *distant* on the difference between *direct* and *indirect* items.

(c) Results

A major difference from the preceding experiment is that the close/distant variable, whether effective or not (which we shall see later), is not in interaction with the originality/deviance variable. However, the written instructions will certainly have made the normative context salient for all the subjects. We consider first the results for the close/distant variable (Table 24).

In this experiment, the minority was presented as an ecology group on the political fringe. The effect on the type of item emerges clearly once more, as we would expect according to the psychosocial identity hypothesis: subjects do not systematically commit themselves to opinions close to the source; if they change at all, it is only on the *indirect* items, where the problem of identification is milder $(F = 34 \cdot 245,\ d.f.$ $1/136;\ P < \cdot 0005)$. The change which occurred, however, was not negligible, since it confirms our prediction: when subjects are explicitly

TABLE 24
Mean opinion change

	Direct	Indirect
ORIGINALITY CONTEXT		
Flexible minority	+0·03	+0·65
Rigid minority	+0·08	+0·79
DEVIANCE CONTEXT		
Flexible minority	+0·16	+0·33
Rigid minority	+0·07	+0·36

given to believe that their answers may be revealing a tendency toward deviance, they change less in the direction of the source than when they believe they are being assessed for tendencies toward originality (interaction between item type and originality/deviance: $F = 7 \cdot 756,\ d.f.\ 1/136;\ P < \cdot 01)$.

We may perhaps regret that the normative context induced did not interact with the flexibilty/rigidity variable, but the absence of such an effect should not surprise us, since the minority character of the influence source had been explicitly identified. We have already shown how such identification alone can "block" even the effects of flexibility.

Nevertheless, we should not conclude that the flexibility/rigidity variable had no effects at all: as we shall see, it played a role in the distribution of opinion changes according to whether subjects were close or distant from the source. This is how we interpret the significant triple interaction $(F = 7 \cdot 262,\ d.f.\ 1/36;\ P < \cdot 01)$ among the three factors in Table 25.

These results can be summarized as follows. First, it is clear that the manipulated variables had no effect on the *indirect* items. It is therefore on the *direct* items that the differentiation between close and distant subjects shows its effect, and in the direction that, theoretically, we would have supposed. Confronted with a rigid text, it is those subjects who were initially closest to the position of the minority who change the least, and even show some negative influence, as if the urgency of disassociating oneself (we are tempted to use the term "dissimilation" like Lemaine *et al.*, 1971–1972, and Lemaine, 1975) were as strong in proportion as the minority position includes elements which identify it precisely as a minority, as pointed out by the experimenter.

TABLE 25
Mean opinion change

	Direct	Indirect
Close subjects/flexible minority	+0·07	+0·38
Close subjects/rigid minority	−0·27	+0·55
Distant subjects/flexible minority	+0·11	+0·61
Distant subjects/rigid minority	+0·42	+0·60

Overall then, these results are consistent with an interpretation of social influence in terms of the redefinition of psychosocial identity in specific situations.

In the penultimate experiment of this series we approached this question of psychosocial identity by a different route. We gave subjects to believe that the text they were reading was designed to select people for membership in a minority group.

Experiment 13: The text as a regulator of group membership

We have borrowed the notion of membership regulation from the recent work of Deconchy (1971, 1980) on religious orthodoxy. In particular, Deconchy studied how the psychosocial regulation of membership operates when a part of the orthodox discourse is called into question. This work therefore shows how the discourse is essential to orthodox subjects' definition and self-definition of their identity. This is a somewhat different area of enquiry, but it emphasizes the relationship of discourse to membership regulation.

This regulatory aspect has been apparent in our experiments, especially when we have interpreted influence behaviours as involving a redefinition of psychosocial identity. If this hypothesis is correct, it should be sufficient to tell subjects that the text they are reading serves a regulatory function in regard to the minority group concerned in order to cause them some difficulty in expressing agreement with, or approach toward, the minority position when it is presented rigidly.

The paradigm used in this experiment has been used before for different purposes (Mugny, 1975b), when we used two xenophobic texts, one consistent and the other inconsistent. Consistency was found to play an essential part, although the extent of influence was not very great. It is important to note that the previous experiment was done at a time when xenophobic policies were being mooted in the country, and we were working in a region with a strong anti-xenophobic tradition, where attitudes were very strongly entrenched. The question of identity, at that time, was posed in somewhat different terms, because it would have been almost impossible, in the social milieu studied, to have expressed xenophobic opinions. This explains the very strong polarization of attitudes which was already evident on pre-test, as well as the zero or even negative influence we obtained on the items most explicitly linked with the discourse. However, times change, and the xenophobia question has receded to admit others to the forefront of concern (ecology, nuclear power, the economic crisis, etc.) even if discrimination on the basis of nationality is still an issue.

In a less emotive situation we used the consistent text as the equivalent of "rigid", and the inconsistent text as the equivalent of "flexible". (A reinterpretation of this experiment in terms of flexibility and rigidity of negotiation is proposed by Riba and Mugny, 1981.) In doing this, we took certain precautions to make sure that the texts really were evaluated in these terms by the subjects. Let us look at the experiment in detail.

(a) Opinion ratings

The opinion questionnaire contained 16 propositions about the presence of foreigners in Switzerland (Table 26). As in the pollution questionnaire, the propositions were organized along several dimensions. The subjects' task was to express the extent of their agreement or dis-

TABLE 26
Questionnaire on opinions toward foreigners (scale illustrated for item 1 only)

1. The only right that should be granted to foreign workers is that of working in our country.

   AGREE   1   2   3   4   5   6   7   8   9   10   11   12   DISAGREE

2. The housing shortage is caused by the immigration of too many foreign workers.

3. It is wrong to accuse immigrant workers of being the main cause of higher prices. They feel the effects of them before we do.

4. The arrival of foreign workers in Switzerland has certainly been responsible for a rise in the crime rate.

5. It is unacceptable for a foreign worker in a firm to receive the same wages as Swiss people.

6. Foreign workers, just the same as Swiss people, often have to live on the outskirts of towns and far from their places of work.

7. Foreign culture and folklore can exist side by side with Swiss culture and folklore without threatening them in any way.

8. The expulsion of foreigners for political reasons must be stopped.

9. Often living in very poor housing conditions, foreign workers suffer as much from the housing shortage as we do, if not more.

10. It is quite normal for foreigners who engage in political activities to be deported.

11. There is no doubt that the presence of foreign workers has caused prices to rise in Switzerland.

12. Foreign workers should have the same political and trade union rights as Swiss citizens.

13. Switzerland's cultural traditions are threatened by foreign immigration.

14. Because there are so many foreign workers, some Swiss people have to live on the outskirts of towns and a long way from their places of work.

15. It is false to claim that the arrival of foreign workers in Switzerland has increased the crime rate.

16. Foreign workers in a firm should have the same opportunities for promotion as Swiss people.

agreement with the propositions on a 12-point scale (1 indicating agreement, and 12 disagreement).

Eight items put forward xenophobic ideas, and 8 were anti-xenophobic. Within each set of eight items, four were directly related to the text. These *direct* items touched on themes raised in the xenophobic text: political and trade union rights, and residence rights. Thus the *direct* items are those accepting or rejecting such rights.

The remaining items referred to cultural and economic issues (such as parity of wages between native and foreign workers). These were the 8 *indirect* items.

We checked for carry-over effects due to including *direct* items within both xenophobic and anti-xenophobic categories. There were very few such instances, so the results are not too distorted by grouping these items together in spite of the fact that the influence source is xenophobic. Influence is positive for the xenophobic items when they are more accepted (or less rejected), and the reverse is the case for the anti-xenophobic items. Similarly for the *indirect* items, which are about dimensions not touched on in the text.

(b) The text

How did the subjects place themselves on these various items? At the time of pre-test the subjects were on average non-xenophobic. This was as expected, given that the experiment was carried out in the same non-xenophobic region as our 1975 experiment. On the 12-point scale, the mean for the xenophobic items was around 9 and around 3 for the non-xenophobic items. In other words, the positions were fairly symmetrical (the distribution on either side of the mid-point of the scale was very similar), and this allows us to treat together the changes on xenophobic or non-xenophobic items, and within these the *direct* or *indirect* items.

One week after filling in the questionnaire, the subjects received a text (Table 27), which they read before filling in the same questionnaire again. These were in fact two versions of the same basic text, which expressed the opposition of the minority group towards foreigners, who were seen as threatening the political, trade union, and housing situation. The minority in this case was reactionary: we are assuming, without evidence to the contrary, that a minority of this kind may be subject to the same kind of mechanisms as the minorities in our previous experiments.

As mentioned, above, one version of the basic text had already been used as a consistent text, and the other as an inconsistent one. To make the text inconsistent, certain paragraphs from the consistent text were modified and placed at the end. The consistent text expressed determination to fight against the influx of foreigners and put forward some examples of discriminations which should be applied. In the

TABLE 27

The texts[a]

For several years, the question of foreign immigration has given rise to a heated debate in Switzerland, and many divided positions have been taken up about it.

More than a million foreigners now live in Switzerland, which means that one resident in five is not Swiss. This has created real problems which are economic and social as much as political.

These problems have not been resolved, and they will not be until certain measures have been taken.

A

Our group has taken a firm stance toward these problems for several years now. We shall continue in the future our efforts to make sure that the social advantages and the political and trade union rights which belong to the Swiss are not extended to foreigners.

The housing crisis

The affluence of foreign workers has brought about a serious housing shortage in our country. New building can no longer meet the demand for apartments created by the needs of so many foreign immigrants. Although it is true that some of these work in the building industry, this should not prevent us from seeing that the housing crisis is basically due to the constant influx of foreigners into our country.

Furthermore, because foreign workers take up all the cheapest accommodation, Swiss families have no option but to accept the more expensive housing on the outskirts of towns, entailing long journeys to work.

B

Good, cheap housing close to the place of work absolutely must be reserved for the Swiss first. We want the Swiss to have priority in the allocation of apartments.

Trade union rights

In Switzerland, foreign workers find not only work that does not exist in their own country but also salaries and a standard of living much better than anything they could expect at home. Foreigners do not need trade union rights, because they already have far greater advantages than they could have in their own country.

C

If immigrants had trade union rights, they could make exaggerated wage claims, put our whole economy in danger, and threaten the interests of Swiss people. In fact, the interests of Swiss workers are different from the interests of foreign workers.

Political rights

It is pointless to give foreigners political rights, because they already have them in their own countries. In any case, we cannot see how foreign political traditions can be compatible with our own, special, and long-established democratic traditions. It could be necessary, for example, to deport foreigners who by their political actions fail to respect the principles of the "oldest democracy in the world".

D

So we should not accept that foreigners can have the same political rights as Swiss people.

---

inconsistent text, these paragraphs about discrimination were replaced by others in which the minority expresses indecision, or even refusal, to implement discriminations which would have followed from the preceding points.

The problem was how to transform consistency/inconsistency into rigidity/flexibility. In seeking a means of doing this, we were inspired by the results of Experiment 6, in which we had induced different images to the same text by attributing these images to fictional previous readers. So in Experiment 13 subjects were asked to read the text in order to form an impression of the marginal group who had produced it. We specified that subjects should give "your impression as to *its suppleness or its rigidity*. Do this by placing a cross next to each adjective which you think corresponds to the degree of *suppleness in the opinions of this minority group*". By emphasizing this aspect of the instructions, we made both the minority character of the source, and the flexibility/rigidity dimension, salient. There followed 10 adjectives taken from the list of 40 in our source-image questionnaire, of which 5 were rigid and 5 flexible: *cooperative, arrogant, authoritarian, open, domineering, agreeable, understanding, stubborn, hostile, sociable*.

An induction of this kind is undoubtedly sufficient to allow us to speak henceforth in terms of a rigid and a flexible text. This manipulation is important for our hypothesis regarding psychosocial identification. The rigid text gives a very firm outline of the positions adopted, with no room for doubt on the part of the reader; the flexible text formulates the same anti-foreigner positions but leaves the outlines of possible affiliation to this group very fluid.

---

[a] The text opposite was used in the *rigid minority* condition. The text for the *flexible minority* condition was obtained by replacing paragraphs A, B, C, and D above with paragraphs A', B', C', and D' respectively.

A'
Our group has never adopted specific positions on these problems. We only attempt to raise the issues surrounding the question of whether we should refuse the social advantages and the political and trade union rights of the Swiss to foreigners.

B'
Good, cheap housing close to the place of work should be reserved first for the Swiss. But we do not think that the Swiss should have priority in the allocation of apartments.

C'
If they had trade union rights, immigrants could, by making exaggerated wage claims, endanger our whole economy and threaten the interests of Swiss people, even though we cannot be certain that the interests of Swiss and foreign workers are different.

D'
But should we refuse all political rights to foreigners? We do not say that.

This was the first variable. The second variable introduces the notion of membership regulation.

(c) Membership regulation

In a *without regulation* condition, no additional information was given to the subjects.

In a *with regulation* condition, the subjects were told that the text they were going to read was used to select people for membership in the minority group. According to our hypotheses, this should have made the question of identification with the source a salient one for the subjects. For half the subjects, then, we added that the text constituted the political programme of the minority group, and that future adherents of the group would have to accept it and sign it in order to become members. Nothing could be more explicit.

(d) Distance from source

Subjects here also divided according to whether they were "close" to or "distant" from the source. As in the preceding experiment, this was according to the degree of acceptance of the xenophobic and non-xenophobic items.

(e) Results

In the interests of clarity we shall give only those results which are related to the difference between *direct* and *indirect* items and which confirm the results we obtained with the pollution paradigm. There was an indication of an interaction between these items and the variable of minority flexibility or rigidity ($F = 3.400$, *d.f.* 1/80; $P < .10$). Further analysis indicates that both types of minority had a roughly equal effect on the *indirect* items ($F = .102$, *d.f.* 1/80), but that the flexible minority had markedly more influence than the rigid minority on the *direct* items ($F = 6.950$, *d.f.* 1/80; $P < 0.25$). Alternatively, it could be said that the flexible minority had the same degree of influence whatever the type of item, while a significant difference appeared for the rigid minority which, as in all the experiments presented previously with various paradigms, manifests very great difficulty in influencing the most socially explicit responses.

A second result confirms our hypothesis that subjects closest to the source would be most resistant to such explicitness. The significant interaction between the type of item and the closeness/distance of the subject ($F = 6{\cdot}067$, d.f. 1/80) reinforces this point; the most distant subjects did not show any difference in influence according to the type of item ($F = 0{\cdot}624$), but the closest subjects manifested less influence on the *direct* items than on the *indirect* ones ($F = 7{\cdot}255$, d.f. 1/80; $P < {\cdot}01$). Thus the subjects initially closest to the source were most susceptible to the experimental variations, as would have been predicted by the notion of social identification being most salient for them.

Considering the variable of the explicitness of membership regulation, Table 28 shows the mean opinion changes for the 8 experimental conditions. At first sight, the results are not very clear. The most distant subjects are particularly insensitive to the experimental variations, although they have slightly higher means where there was no membership regulation ($F = 2{\cdot}290$, d.f. 1/80).

TABLE 28
Mean opinion changes

	Close	Distant
Flexible minority/without regulation	+0·12	+0·93
Flexible minority/with regulation	+1·67	+0·55
Rigid minority/without regulation	+0·74	+0·88
Rigid minority/with regulation	−0·30	+0·36

With close subjects things are clearer: as predicted, there is a significant interaction between the two first-order factors ($F = 6{\cdot}970$, d.f. 1/80; $P < 0{\cdot}25$). Making explicit the membership question led to a clear rejection of the rigid minority positions. However, there was also an interesting effect: when the issue of membership is made explicit in relation to a flexible text, influence is manifested very strongly—in fact most strongly of all the experimental conditions.

Thus the importance of social identity and its redefinition in social influence situations emerges clearly, and in various manifestations, in this experiment. First, we see once again that the greatest blockages against influence appear on those items most directly associated with the minority discourse, in other words on items that raise most explicitly the question of the redefinition of social identity. Next, it was those subjects closest to the source (or, in fact, less distant) for whom this difference in influence according to the type of item was greatest. Finally, and not surprisingly, the question of membership and hence of the redefinition of membership was important for subjects closest to the minority position. If the minority is rigid and strictly regulates its membership, its influence diminishes considerably (as predicted). The risk of social identification with such a position, which had particularly negative connotations in this experiment, was too great for these subjects.

It is curious that when the minority is flexible and lays down no conditions for membership, its influence greatly increases. This effect could reveal itself to be very important. It suggests that our hypothesis concerning membership regulation must be modified to take account of the possibility that this variable may strongly convince (by its absence), in addition to creating strong resistance to influence when it is present. In particular, there is an interaction between this variable and the behavioural style of the minority. When the minority is flexible, it is more influential, because the situational context legitimates its flexibility or at least makes its flexibility salient.

This last point, finally, does not contradict our previous findings. It is true that we have been concerned with the conditions which could lead to the removal of barriers to the diffusion of innovation by a rigid source and that we have also demonstrated the factors which can, in the same situations, prevent the usual positive effects of a flexible minority. This last experiment perhaps serves to indicate the conditions which, in contrast, may facilitate these positive effects.

Experiment 14: Influence and shared category membership

Social influence consists in the redefinition of psychosocial identity, and this means that to move toward an influence source involves not only adapting one's response on the issue with which the influence relationship is concerned but also taking on all, or some of, the stereotypical characteristics of the source. For ideological reasons that we have already discussed, subjects generate a negative image (dominated by the dimension of rigid blockage of negotiation) of a minority source which is recognized as such. To make an explicit approach to this source would be tantamount to attributing negative characteristics to oneself. This is how we have interpreted a number of findings that have impressed us with their systematic nature. Thus, the influence of a rigid, or explicitly minority source is null (when it is not negative) on those items most directly associated with the source's explicit responses. Furthermore, it is those subjects already most polarized in their opinions who manifest least influence, and this becomes more true as the situation makes the question of social identity more salient.

This is also how we have interpreted the several instances in which a rigid minority, categorized as dogmatic, has had very little influence. We have argued that the perceived rigidity of minority behaviours serves to define the limits of minority positions (positions which are necessarily more extreme than those held in the population studied) with such clarity that subjects have no difficulty in perceiving themselves as totally excluded from the minority group, and so because the minority is perceived as belonging to a different group (even to the group of *the different*), this differentiation at the level of representation will easily be translated into the behavioural and evaluative differentiations that we have seen.

The final experiment asks: if the effects of rigidity arise from the representation of self-exclusion from the minority group, is it then possible to prevent these effects by making salient, instead, a shared category identification with the minority? If subjects receive a rigid text from a source with whom they share the same category membership, these intra-category similarities should lead to stronger identifications at the level of behaviour and evaluation. More specifically, the social influence resulting should be greater.

As in previous experiments, we could also advance the hypothesis that the influence of the more flexible minority should be less sensitive to the salience of these common memberships. The effects of a flexible source can be described in a corollary fashion: by means of its flexibility, the flexible minority source should make such shared memberships salient (more or less implicitly) or at least should avoid having its positions too firmly categorized. By extension, it is possible to interpret flexible styles as making explicit crossed memberships (Deschamps, 1977) which would attenuate the effects of a simple categorization.

The experiment we carried out consisted in leading subjects to think that they either had few shared category memberships with the minority or that they had many shared category memberships.

THE EXPERIMENT

More than one hundred subjects took part in this final experiment. There were two experimental sessions, separated by a week. In the first session, subjects responded to the usual questionnaire about the responsibility for pollution, but this time using an 11-point scale (instead of a 7-point one). One week later, they read the usual minority text (with flexible or rigid slogans) and filled in the opinion questionnaire once more.

The experimental design included three independent variables.

(1) The minority text included either flexible or rigid slogans.

(2) The subjects were either close to, or distant from, the minority source. The criteria used to establish this were the same as those in Experiment 10: subjects were divided into the two categories as a function of the difference in their acceptance of *direct* and *indirect* items.

(3) The subjects were told that they had a number of category memberships (either 1 or 5, out of a possible total of 8) in common with the minority source (see below).

To obtain an equal number of subjects in each of the 8 conditions created by the combination of these three variables, some subjects were discarded at random. The final total was 104 subjects, 13 in each experimental condition.

The central experimental variable in this experiment was the induction of belief in the subjects that they shared few, or many, category memberships with the minority source. To achieve this, we gave the subjects instructions. The first paragraph was the same for all subjects, thus adding verisimilitude to the instructions:

> Every individual can be defined according to whether or not they belong to certain very general social categories: everyone must be either a man or a woman; either young or not young; either an intellectual worker or a manual worker; either a student or an employee.

The next two paragraphs differed according to the experimental condition. In the condition *one common membership*, the question put to subjects was:

Analysis of your social origin and that of the authors of the text you are going to read reveals that of the 8 categories below, only 1 (or at the most 2 according to the individual case) is common to both you and the text authors. Try to guess intuitively what category this is, on the basis of your reading of the text.

After reading the text, answer by putting a cross (**X**) next to the single proposition (or two, at the most) that you agree to, i.e. the single category you think you have in common with the authors of the text.

In the condition *five common memberships*, the question was:

Analysis of your social origin and that of the authors of the text you are going to read reveals that of the 8 categories below, you have 5 (or in some cases 6) in common with the text authors. Try to guess intuitively which these are, on the basis of your reading of the text.

After reading the text, answer by putting a cross (**X**) next to the 5 (or 6) propositions with which you agree, i.e. the 5 (or 6) categories you think you have in common with the authors of the text.

In the two conditions, subjects had to choose one or more category memberships they held in common with the influence source, by indicating which of the following 8 propositions they accepted as having in common:

We are intellectuals.
We belong to the same sex.
We are members of an ecological group.
We are receiving a religious education.
We are young.
We are members of a political party.
We come from a privileged social background.
We are students (in the broadest sense).

Most of the common memberships proposed are plausible: most of the subjects were young students from a privileged background, men, and members of a religious college.

It can also be reasonably claimed that the formulation in the *one common membership* condition made the rarity of this commonality of membership salient, but that in the *five common memberships* condition made the large area of shared membership salient.

It is also important to emphasize that, to be plausible in the experimental manipulation, the social categories proposed allowed no inferences to be drawn as to specific opinions. The only categories which could have been relevant in this respect were "ecological group" and "political party", and it was highly probable that subjects would not choose these. Therefore, if any effects were obtained, they would be due to the act of categorization alone.

Results

Did the subjects accept the number of shared social categories between themelves and the influence source to which we had assigned them? In general, the answer is yes. In the *one common membership* condition, subjects gave a mean response of 1·67. In the *five common memberships* condition, however, the instructions were followed less systematically: the mean response was 3·85, indicating that a certain amount of conflict was occurring.

It is also interesting to note that in the *five common memberships* conditions a difference appeared between "close" and "distant" subjects. The close subjects gave a mean of 4·31 shared memberships; the subjects most distant from the minority opinions gave a mean of 3·38. This result serves to validate our manipulation of the close/distant variable, incidentally.

The flexibility/rigidity variable, on the other hand, did not show itself at the level of this particular measure. It would appear that the induction of one or more shared category memberships was particularly effective. It should be emphasized that once the identification of category membership(s) had taken place, it gave rise to two inverse effects. In the *one common membership* condition, it diminished the effect of flexibility (which of itself implies more shared category memberships than rigidity); conversely, it increases the effect of rigidity in the *five common memberships* condition.

Let us now consider how these effects were related to social influence. Taking general points first of all, there were the usual effects of *direct* and *indirect* items, although these were not in interaction with any of the other variables. More strikingly there was an overall effect of the number of common memberships ($F = 3·646$, *d.f.* 1/96; $P < ·06$). Influence is greater as the number of shared memberships with the source rises.

Although the flexibility/rigidity variable by itself has no significant effect, rigidity does strongly interact with the effects of the number of shared memberships ($F = 5·038$, *d.f.* 1/96; $P < ·03$), the difference being not significant for the flexible condition (for which the F is smaller than 1). Our hypothesis is therefore supported.

Finally, the number of common memberships variable is in interaction with the close/distant variable ($F = 3·466$, $d.f.$ 1/96; $P < ·07$). Once again, the effect of the induction was especially strong in the case of those subjects already close to the minority source.

Because the effects are particularly clear for the condition with a rigid text, we give details for this condition only (Table 29)—accepting, therefore, that the effects were much weaker with a flexible text, although these were in the same direction. (It should be recalled that the rating scale for this experiment had 11 points.)

TABLE 29
Mean opinion change (rigid condition only)

	Direct	Indirect
One common membership/close subjects	−0·93	+0·86
One common membership/distant subjects	+0·16	+1·47
Five common memberships/close subjects	+0·13	+1·84
Five common memberships/distant subjects	+0·43	+1·71

Apart from the strong impact of the number of shared memberships in this rigid condition, the most striking effect in this experiment is the significant negative influence on subjects close to a source with whom they have only a single shared membership ($t = 2·86$, $d.f.$ 12; $P < ·02$). Although the fact that subjects closest to the source changed less is hardly surprising (is not the conflict for them less severe, or at least would we not expect it to be *a priori*?), the fact that the change which took place was in a negative direction is more striking. What is happening here is not simply a diminution of influence but a different process altogether, an active mechanism of dissimilation (Lemaine, 1975), a search for self-differentiation where the possibility arises of a confusion of one's own identity with that of the minority group. Furthermore, this is one of the rare instances of negative influence in our experiments. The salience of a single shared membership revealed not only the refusal to identify with the source but also the search for dissimilation.

This experiment therefore confirms that one of the reasons why the minority (especially when rigid) encounters obstacles in its attempts to influence arises from the fact that subjects see it as an out-group with which they have nothing in common. This categorization brings about evaluative discriminations (of the sort we have found throughout this research) and also behavioural discriminations (considering as behaviours the judgements emitted by the source relative to the object in question).

With a flexible source, these effects are less strong. This is not surprising: as we have seen, the categorization of a flexible minority is more equivocal and allows the recognition of several shared memberships. These common memberships serve to attenuate the discriminations evoked by categorization of the minority as such.

These results confirm that influence relations are embedded within a context of group relationships and that social influence is a matter of re-defining social identity within this framework of group relations. It may be objected that the social categories introduced into this experiment were not directly relevant to, or necessary for, the definition of a minority's stance. However, categorizations are never necessary for the identification of any opinion, and although this may be the case logically or "rationally", from the psychosociological point of view things are quite otherwise, as also from the ideological point of view as we have demonstrated in previous experiments. The mechanisms of naturalization must also be understood in this way, since this is the dominant mode in which active minorities are categorized, namely by having stereotypical characteristics associated with them, as we have seen.

Finally, it is worth noting that certain propositions of Moscovici's (1976, p. 147) are confirmed by these results; for instance, that rigidity may well be an effective style in the context of intragroup relations, while flexibility may be effective rather in intergroup relations, when the minority is attempting to win over people who are not already members of the minority. There are, moreover, several political parties which have recommended these various styles as strategies, almost as dogmas, to be directed either "internally" or "externally". Other social movements, for reasons proper to them (pursuit of cohesion, renunciation of opportunism), seem to blend the two. In this case, they run the risk of being strongly admired by some, but rejected by many others, through the operation of the mechanisms which this research has attempted to demonstrate.

Conclusions

Now that our psychosociological theory of the influence of minorities has been described in detail and illustrated experimentally, we can proceed to draw out the principal conclusions, from the point of view of verification of the theory itself, the links between the theory and the methodology, and the relationship of the theory to social psychology in general.

A definition was proposed of social psychology as a study that articulates the models which are appropriate at different levels of analysis. The introduction showed how various levels of analysis have been privileged in social psychology (the levels of the individual and of interpersonal relations) while others have been largely ignored (such as the level of relations between groups or social categories, and above all the level of ideology). Our approach to the study of minority influence tried to show how, in relation to one specific subject (though an extremely important one in social relations), an analysis which aims to be exhaustive must focus on the mechanisms which arise from the articulation of these various levels upon each other. To do this, certain privileged axes have been selected for special attention.

This study has focused throughout flexible or rigid influence strategies that define the relationship between minority or minorities and the population "at stake".

These social influence relations have been placed within a context of social conflict in which pressures toward innovation or social change, themselves meet opposing pressures toward uniformity.

Naturalization as an ideological mode of perception of minorities has emerged as a dominant mechanism in the efforts by power to mask the existence of social antagonisms and hence, *a fortiori*, the existence of power relations themselves.

Finally, the proposal of the notion of social identification has allowed us to articulate together the "individual" acceptance of minority positions, relations between groups, and ideological mechanisms.

Let us now try to summarize these various articulations.

Moscovici's (1976) consistency theory has shown the conditions in which minorities, lacking power *a priori*, are able nevertheless to break the social consensus by means of the consistency and firmness of their behaviour. Consistency, in fact, defines the nature of the antagonistic stance adopted by the minority toward power. The blockage of negotiation with power can cause the minority to be perceived as being totally opposed. However, we have also seen that the population itself is not without a relationship toward power: it is in fact "subject" to power, in a dominance relationship which is sometimes ideological and sometimes repressive. The minority's own conflict with power, which defines its consistency, almost inevitably brings about an additional conflict between minority and population. For any positive influence to take place, this conflict must be negotiated; a rigid minority, extending its failure to negotiate with power to its relation with the population, tends to make its positions difficult to accept. This is a prime axis of articulation: the problem of the diffusion of minority innovation needs to be re-situated within a sociological context of group relations in which minority behaviours take place and have specific meanings; the groups concerned are the "majority" (differentiated into power and population) and the minority. These group relations have a determining effect on minority influence in two ways: first, via the ideological productions which determine the population's perception and representation of the minority, secondly, via the notion of social identity.

The psychosociological mechanisms of minority influence are situated at the level of the population's representation of the source. This in turn depends on the conflict relationship between population and minority: thus minority rigidity will mean that behavioural characteristics relevant to the blockage of negotiation will be most salient in the population's perception of the minority. These characteristics will contaminate the perception of minority consistency which would otherwise ensure a positive influence effect. But these characteristics only affect minority influence through the intervention of ideological mechanisms, one of which consists in interpreting minority behaviours as arising from "natural" characteristics of the minority. In the experimental situations we have considered, the postulation of such a mechanism was necessary to understand the regularity of rigidity effects. By means of *ad hoc* experimental interventions we were able to prevent the activation of this mechanism, thus confirming that the mechanism is indeed tied to group relations. Its function appears to be to neutralize the possible influence of deviant minorities in a non-repressive manner. The effects of rigidity like those of flexibility, are not merely a matter of interpersonal relations but are articulated with complex mechanisms arising out of much more general relationships among groups.

Once this point has been made, the question arises as to the role of the social sciences—especially psychiatry, psychology, and social psychology—in the institutionalized forms of these ideological modes of treatment of social deviance in the broadest sense. (Although we have an opinion on this question, we shall not dwell on it here; it requires separate systematic study.)

Recent studies of intergroup relations (Tajfel, 1978, 1981; Tajfel and Turner, 1979) have brought to light the importance of the notion of social identity. By means of their identifications with social groups and categories, individuals define their own identity. The extension of this hypothesis to influence relations was not difficult: approach or avoidance behaviours in relation to an influence source can easily be translated into a matter of redefinition of social identity in a specific context. To be influenced by a source is to identify oneself at least partially with it and to attribute to oneself the stereotypical characteristics of the group or category. These identifications take place within the framework of intergroup relations. As far as minority influence specifically is concerned, it is easy to see how the explicit recognition of ideological stigmatization of the minority source would prevent the possible influence of minorities. Since influence consists of a redefinition of social identity, the influence process would meet the difficulty that stereotypical characteristics of the minority (in this case negative characteristics) would necessarily have to be attributed to themselves by the population. Yet we can also imagine social contexts in which the intervention of these negative characteristics could be prevented. We have shown that appeal to a norm of social change, or focusing on a purely political dimension of the minority, can reverse this difficulty into a facilitation. Thus the minority may manage to place its aims on the historical agenda, and thereby attract individuals who value their minority identification. In a similar fashion rigidity can attain more influence when subjects are led to perceive that they have several category memberships in common with the minority.

Minorities, then, are sometimes able to place their aims on the agenda of history. What are these aims? Sometimes they are the same as those of part or even all of what we have called the population. And the realization of these aims is dependent, not only on acts of power, but also of the population, who may find in the minority the expression, even the stereotypical expression, of their own aims.

This articulated conception of the processes by which minority influence may or may not affect a whole society, escapes the reductionism that characterizes the traditional study of social influence processes. We have not had to reduce these to simple personal variables, for instance arising out of personality traits, any more than we have had to reduce them to simple inter-individual negotiations. The mechanisms revealed by this type of analysis have been placed in systematic relation to the mechanisms of intergroup relations, together with the ideology whose essential function is to mask the asymmetry between groups. This conception has rested on the possibility, and the results of, experimental verification.

In our introduction, we emphasized that a science is not defined by its methodology. We can add as a corollary that a science should not be stigmatized on grounds of its methodology alone. Social psychology, we are convinced, has not been criticized (and deservedly) because it is experimental, but because the levels of explanation it has confined itself to have not ventured beyond intra-individual, intra-situational, or inter-individual variables. We have therefore conserved an experimental approach which seemed to us adequate for the object of study—the influence of minorities—but we have also and more importantly attempted to integrate certain dimensions, which we would term historical, into our explanations and *a fortiori* into our paradigms. (This is not to imply that we consider other approaches, which we ourselves do not practice, to be inadequate to a similar purpose.) It should be noted, however, that here one is not doing what might be termed historical social psychology—that would merely be the study of social events in the past. The events occurring in our paradigms are historical only because they are contemporary and are part of the social changes that will mark our epoch and our society. We intend our work also as an argument in favour of experimentation in social psychology, which in our opinion has been too often condemned for reasons which are in reality not to do with its methodology at all.

Social psychology is often called into question. If it is not being accused of providing the scientific legitimation for the dominant ideology, then the artificiality of the situations it sets up for the study of social objects is being attacked. Our study of the phenomena of minority influence is intended to show at least that neither of these charges are necessarily true, even though they are true of a number of approaches (perhaps the majority of approaches) which are characterized by the fact that in their explanations they reduce the social phenomena they are studying to mechanisms of a purely psychological or interpersonal order. This happens to social psychology through the operation of the same ideological mechanisms we have seen in action in some of our experiments: at this level we can speak of institutionalized psychologization and psychosociologization.

Although we accept (actively) many of the criticisms made against social psychology, we also insist that there is a danger of throwing the baby out with the bathwater. We must not lose the opportunity to grasp the mechanisms which, at several levels, modulate social phenomena and which relate in a *non-mechanistic* fashion the individual and the social, the contemporary and the historial. It would be reductionist, even idealist, to ignore such an opportunity.

Our approach has attempted to avoid all reductionism by approaching the phenomena of minority social influence with an articulated viewpoint, trying to discern the mechanisms at levels ranging from the individual to the social totality which would enable us to understand these phenomena within the social context they inhabit. In doing so, we have not ceased to be psychosociologists, rather we have tried to define an alternative way of doing social psychology.

References

Allen, V. L. (1965). Situational factors in conformity. *In* Berkowitz, L. (ed.), *Advances in experimental social psychology* II, pp. 133–175. Academic Press, New York and London.

Allen, V. L. (1975). Social support for nonconformity. *In* Berkowitz, L. (ed.), *Advances in experimental social psychology* VIII. Academic Press, New York and London.

Althusser, L. (1976). *Positions*. Editions sociales, Paris.

Apfelbaum, E. and Herzlich, C. (1970/1971). La théorie de l'attribution en psychologie sociale, *Bulletin de Psychologie* 24, 961–976.

Asch, S. E. (1951). Effects of group pressure upon the modification and distortion of judgement. *In* Guetzkow, H. (ed.), *Groups, leadership and men*. Carnegie Press, Pittsburgh.

Asch, S. E. (1952). *Social psychology*. Prentice-Hall, Englewood Cliffs, New Jersey.

Asch, S. E. (1956). Studies on independence and conformity: a minority of one against a unanimous majority, *Psychological Monographs* 70, 416.

Bourdieu, P. (1973). L'opinion publique n'existe pas, *Temps Modernes* 29, **318**, 1292–1309.

Brehm, J. W. (1966). *A theory of psychological reactance*. Academic Press, New York and London.

Brehm, J. W. and Mann, M. (1975). Effects of importance of freedom and attraction to group members on influence produced by group pressure, *Journal of Personality and Social Psychology* **31**, 816–824.

Crutchfield, R. S. (1955). Conformity and character, *American Psychologist* **10**, 5, 191–198.

Deconchy, J. P. (1971). *L'orthodoxie religieuse. Essai de logique psycho-sociale*. Editions ouvrières, Paris.

Deconchy, J. P. (1980). *Orthodoxie religieuse et sciences humaines*. Mouton, La Haye.

Deschamps, J. C. (1977). *L'attribution et la catégorisation sociale*. Lang, Berne.

Doise, W. (1978a). Images, représentations, idéologies et expérimentations psychosociologiques, *Social Science Information* **17**, 1, 41–69.

Doise, W. (1978b). *Groups and individuals*. Cambridge University Press, Cambridge.

Doise, W. (1982). *L'explication en psychologie sociale*. Presses Universitaires de France, Paris.

Doise, W., Deschamps, J. C. and Mugny, G. (1978). *Psychologie sociale expérimentale*. Armand Colin, Paris.

Doise, W. and Moscovici, S. (1969–1970). Approche et évitement du déviant dans des groupes de cohésion différente, *Bulletin de Psychologie* **23**, 522–525.

Doms, M. (1978). *Moscovici's innovatie-effekt: poging tot integratie met het conformisme-effekt*. Doctoral dissertation, Leuven.

Doms, M. and Van Avermaet, E. (1980a). Majority influence, minority influence and conversion effect: a replication, *Journal of Experimental Social Psychology* **16**, 283–292.

Doms, M. and Van Avermaet, E. (1980b). *Social support and minority influence: the innovation effect reconsidered*. International symposium on social influence processes, Barcelona.

Eiser, J. R. and Pancer, S. M. (1979). Attitudinal effects of the use of evaluatively biased language. *European Journal of Social Psychology* **9**, 1, 39–47.

Eiser, J. R. and Ross, M. A. (1977). Partisan language, immediacy and attitude change, *European Journal of Social Psychology* **7**, 4, 477–489.

Eiser, J. R. and Stroebe, W. (1972). *Categorisation and social judgment*. Academic Press, New York and London.

Faucheux, C. and Moscovici, S. (1967). Le style de comportement d'une minorité et son influence sur les réponses d'une majorité, *Bulletin du C.E.R.P.* **16**, 337–360.

Flament, C. (1959a). Modèle stratégique des processus d'influence sociale sur les jugements perceptifs, *Psychologie Française* 91–101.

Flament, C. (1959b). Ambiguïté du stimulus, incertitude de la réponse et processus d'influence sociale, *Année Psychologique* **59**, 73–91.

Freedman, J. L. and Doob, A. N. (1968). *Deviancy: the psychology of being different*. Academic Press, New York and London.

French, J. R. (1956). A formal theory of social power, *Psychological Review* **63**, 181–194.

Gough, H. G. (1960). The adjective check list as a personality assessment research technique, *Psychological Reports* **6**, 107–122.

Grounauer, M. M. (1977). *L'affaire Ziegler, Procès d'un hérétique*. Editions Grounauer, Geneva.

Heilman, M. E. (1976). Oppositional behavior as a function of influence attempt intensity and retaliation threat, *Journal of Personality and Social Psychology* **33**, 5, 574–578.

Hollander, E. P. (1960). Competence and conformity in the acceptance of influence, *Journal of Abnormal and Social Psychology* **61**, 360–365.

Hollander, E. P. (1977). Leadership and social exchange processes. *In* Gergen, K. J., Greenberg, M. S. and Willis, R. H. (ed.), *Social exchange theory*. Wiley, New York.

Kelley, H. H. (1967). Attribution theory in social psychology. *In* Levine, L. (ed.), *Nebraska Symposium Motivation*. University of Nebraska Press, Lincoln.

Kelman, H. C. (1958). Compliance, identification, and internalization, three processes of attitude change, *Journal of Conflict Resolution* **2**, 51–60.

Kiesler, C. A. and Pallak, M. S. (1975). Minority influence: the effect of majority reactionaries and defectors, and minority and majority compromisers, upon majority opinion and attraction, *European Journal of Social Psychology* **5**, 237–256.

Kimball, R. K. and Hollander, E. P. (1974). Independence in the presence of an experienced but deviate group member, *Journal of Social Psychology* **93**, 281–292.

Larsen, K. S. (1974). Social cost, belief incongruence and race. Experiments in choice behavior, *Journal of Social Psychology* **94**, 253–267.

Lemaine, G. (1975). Dissimilation and differential assimilation in social influence (situations of "normalization"), *European Journal of Social Psychology* **5**, 1, 93–120.

Lemaine, G., Lasch, E. and Ricateau, P. (1971–1972). L'influence sociale et les systèmes d'action: les effets d'attraction et de répulsion dans une expérience de normalisation avec l'"allocinétique", *Bulletin de Psychologie* **25**, 482–493.

Maier, N. R. F. and McRay, E. P. (1972). Increasing innovation in change situations through leadership skills, *Psychological Reports* **31**, 343–354.

McGuire, W. J. (1969). The nature of attitudes and attitude change. *In* Lindzey, G. and Aronson, E. (ed.), *The handbook of social psychology IV*, pp. 136–314 (2nd edit.).

Merton, R. K. (1957). *Social theory and social structure*. Free Press, New York.

Montmollin, G. (de) (1977). *L'influence sociale: phénomènes, facteurs et théories*. Presses Universitaires de France, Paris.

Moscovici, S. (1972). L'homme en interaction: machine à répondre ou machine à inférer? *In* Moscovici, S. (ed.), *Introduction à la psychologie sociale I*, pp. 59–81. Larousse, Paris.

Moscovici, S. (1976). *Social influence and social change*. Academic Press, London and New York.

Moscovici, S. (1980). Toward a theory of conversion behavior. In Berkowitz, L. (ed.), *Advances in experimental social psychology XIII*, pp. 209–239.

Moscovici, S. and Lage, E. (1978). Studies in social influence in a context of originality judgments. *European Journal of Social Psychology* **8**, 349–365.

Moscovici, S., Lage, E. and Naffrechoux, M. (1969). Influence of a consistent minority on the responses of a majority in a color perception task, *Sociometry* **32**, 365–379.

Moscovici, S., Mugny, G. and Papastamou, S. (1981). "Sleeper effect" et/ou effet minoritaire? Etude théorique et expérimentale de l'influence sociale à retardement, *Cahiers de Psychologie Cognitive* **1**, 199–221.

Moscovici, S. and Personnaz, B. (1980). Studies in social influence, V. Minority influence and conversion behaviour in a perceptual task, *Journal of Experimental Social Psychology* **16**, 270–282.

Moscovici, S. and Ricateau, P. (1972). Conformité, minorité et influence sociale. *In* Moscovici, S., *Introduction à la psychologie sociale I*, pp. 139–191. Larousse, Paris.

Mugny, G. (1974). *Négociations et influence minoritaire*. Doctoral dissertation, mimeo.

Mugny, G. (1975a). Negotiations, image of the other and the process of minority influence, *European Journal of Social Psychology* **5**, 2, 209–228.

Mugny, G. (1975b). Bedeutung der Konsistenz bei der Beeinflussung durch eine kon-
kordante oder diskordante minderheitliche Kommunikation bei sozialen Beur-
teilungsobjeckten, *Zeitschrift für Sozialpsychologie* **6**, 324–332.

Mugny, G. (1979). A rejoinder to Paicheler: the influence of reactionary minorities,
European Journal of Social Psychology **9**, **2**, 223–225.

Mugny, G. and Doise, W. (1979). Niveaux d'analyse dans l'étude expérimentale des
processus d'influence sociale, *Social Science Information* **18**, 819–876.

Mugny, G. and Papastamou, S. (1975–1976). A propos du "crédit idiosynchrasique"
chez Hollander: conformisme initial ou négociation? *Bulletin de Psychologie* **XXIX**
325, **18**, 970–976.

Mugny, G. and Papastamou, S. (1980). When rigidity does not fail: individualization
and psychologization as resistances to the diffusion of minority innovations, *European Journal of Social Psychology* **10**, 43–61.

Mugny, G., Pierrehumbert, B. and Zubel, R. (1972–1973). Le style d'interaction
comme facteur de l'influence sociale, *Bulletin de Psychologie* **26**, **14–16**, 789–793

Mugny, G., Rilliet, D. and Papastamou, S. (1981). Influence minoritaire et identification sociale dans des contextes d'originalité et de déviance, *Revue Suisse de
Psychologie* **4**, 314–332.

Nemeth, C. and Endicott, J. (1976). The midpoint as an anchor: another look at discrepancy of position and attitude change, *Sociometry* **39**, **1**, 11–18.

Nemeth, C., Swedlund, M. and Kanki, B. (1974). Patterning of the minority's
responses and their influence on the majority. *European Journal of Social Psychology* **4**,
1, 53–64.

Nemeth, C. and Wachtler, J. (1973). Consistency and modification of judgment, *Journal of Experimental Social Psychology* **9**, 65–79.

Nemeth, C. and Wachtler, J. (1974). Creating the perceptions of consistency and confidence: a necessary condition for minority influence, *Sociometry* **37**, **4**, 529–540.

Paicheler, G. (1976). Norms and attitude change I: polarization and styles of
behaviour, *European Journal of Social Psychology* **6**, **4**, 405–427.

Paicheler, G. (1977). Norms and attitude change II: the phenomenon of bipolariza-
tion, *European Journal of Social Psychology* **7**, **1**, 5–14.

Papastamou, S., Mugny, G. and Kaiser, C. (1980). Echec à l'influence minoritaire: la
psychologisation, *Recherches de Psychologie Sociale* **2**, 41–56.

Personnaz, B. (1975–1976). Conformité, consensus et référents clandestins, *Bulletin de
Psychologie* **29**, 230–242.

Personnaz, B. (1979). Niveau de résistance à l'influence de réponses nomiques et
anomiques. Etude des phénomènes de référents clandestins et de conversion,
Recherches en Psychologie Sociale **1**, 5–27.

Riba, D. and Mugny, G. (1981). Consistencia y rigidez: reinterpretacion, *Cuadernos de
psicologia*.

Ricateau, P. (1971). Processus de catégorisation d'autrui et les mécanismes d'influence sociale, *Bulletin de Psychologie* **24**, 909–919.

Schachter, S. (1951). Deviation, rejection and communication, *Journal of Abnormal and
Social Psychology* **46**, 190–207.

Sherif, M. (1935). A study of some social factors in perception, *Archives of Psychology*
187.

Sherif, M. and Hovland, C. L. (1965). *Social judgments, assimilation and contrast effects in
communications and attitude change.* Yale University Press, New Haven.

Sherif, M. and Sherif, C. W. (1969). *Social psychology.* Harper and Row, New York.

Siegel, S. (1956). *Non-parametric statistics for the behavioral sciences.* McGraw-Hill, Tokyo.

Sperling, H. G. (1946). An experimental study of some psychological factors in judgment. Master's thesis, New School for social research. Resumed In Asch, S. E. (ed., 1952), *Social psychology*. Prentice-Hall, Englewood Cliffs, New Jersey.

Strodbeck, F. L. and Hook, L. H. (1961). The social dimensions of a twelve-man jury table, *Sociometry* **24**, 397–415.

Tajfel, H. (1978). *Differentiation between social groups: studies in the social psychology of intergroup relations*. Academic Press, London and New York.

Tajfel, H. (1981). *Human groups and social categories: Studies in social psychology*. Cambridge, Cambridge University Press.

Tajfel, H. and Turner, J. C. (1979). An integrative theory of intergroup conflict. *In* W. G. Austin and S. Worchel (ed.), *The social psychology of intergroup relations*. Monterey, Calif., Brooks/Cole.

Tuddenham, R. D. (1961). The influence upon judgement of the apparent discrepancy between self and others, *Journal of Social Psychology* **53**, 69–79.

Turner, J. C. (1981). Towards a cognitive redefinition of the social group, *Cahiers de Psychologie Cognitive* **1**, 93–118.

Wicklund, R. A. (1974). *Freedom and reactance*. Lawrence Erlbaum Ass. Publishers, Potomac, Md.

Winer, B. J. (1962). *Statistical principles in experimental design*. McGraw-Hill, New York.

Zavalloni, M. and Cook, S. W. (1965). Influence of judges' attitudes on ratings of favorableness of statements about a social group, *Journal of Personality and Social Psychology* **1**, 43–54.

Ziegler, J. (1976). *Une Suisse au-dessus de tout soupçon*. Seuil, Paris.

Author index

Subject index